S [ ]
$\equiv$ OF $\equiv$
METAPHYSICS
M A S T E R Y

3 BOOKS IN 1

**Life Changing Truths For Unconventional Thinkers:
The Ultimate Collection To Abundance, Prosperity,
Financial Success, Wealth and Well-Being Using
Metaphysics, The Law Of Attraction And
Manifestation**

Including 18 Do-It-Yourself Energy Experiments

Erik Tao

SECRETS OF METAPHYSICS MASTERY

3 BOOKS IN 1

Life Changing Truths For Unconventional Thinkers:

The Ultimate Collection To Abundance, Prosperity, Financial Success, Wealth and Well-Being Using Metaphysics, The Law Of Attraction And Manifestation

-

Including 18 Do-It-Yourself Energy Experiments

By Erik Tao

Get My Another Book for Free

I want to thank you for purchasing my book and offer you another of my books: "Meditation for Beginners: An extraordinary Guide to Inner Freedom, Happiness and Clarity" (2nd edition) completely free.

Click on the link below to download it:

http://eepurl.com/dfwNyP

Tempted to give up on your meditation goals? Don't let it prevent you from realizing your full potential.

Download the book now

and learn how to keep going.

http://eepurl.com/dfwNyP

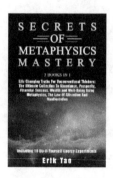

SECRETS OF METAPHYSICS MASTERY:

Life Changing Truths For Unconventional Thinkers

Copyright © 2019 by Erik Tao

All rights reserved. No part of this book may be reproduced in any form including photocopy, scanning or otherwise without prior permission of the copyright holder.

21 METAPHYSICAL SECRETS

Life Changing Truths For Unconventional Thinkers: Including 9 Do-It-Yourself Energy Experiments

Table of Contents:

Introduction

There is a famous Indian fable where six blind men come across an elephant. The first blind man feels its massive side and tells the others that an elephant is like a wall. The second blind man feels the elephant's tusk and reports to the others that an elephant is like a spear. The third blind man encounter's the elephant's trunk and informs the others that an elephant is like a snake. The fourth blind man feels the leg of the elephant and reports that an elephant is like a tree. The fifth blind man encounters the elephant's ear and indicates to the others that an elephant is like a fan. The sixth blind man touches the elephant's tail and states that an elephant is like a rope.

The fable of the blind men and the elephant is a metaphor for how we experience reality. What we refer to as "reality" or the "real world" is based on our sensory abilities, our socialization, and our beliefs. Based on these factors, we believe that our experience of reality is the "true" reality. Each of the blind men in the fable had an experience with the elephant and came away from it with a partial truth; however, the truth of the elephant was missed by all of them. By relying on our beliefs and limited sensory acuity, our perception of reality can be distorted, just as with the blind men.

All conflict among our species is the result of us experiencing life differently. Each person's experience of life is unique, and each person believes that they are experiencing the "real world." There is no challenge that we can face, individually or collectively, that we cannot transcend by changing our perspective. The higher the level of awareness we achieve, the more perspectives that we apply to our lives.

When we can live from different perspectives, we experience greater happiness and freedom. We are not confined to the narrow band of experiences by which most of humanity lives their lives. The purpose of this book is to expose you to different perspectives. By opening yourself up to these different perspectives, you can cultivate a deeper awareness of the nature of reality as well as apply them to your life in a practical way.

When we can embrace the so-called metaphysical world and the "real world," we become intentional participants in the evolution of the human species. The "evolution" that I speak of is the evolution of consciousness, which is the ultimate expression of love.

What is Metaphysics?

Metaphysics is the philosophy that deals with the origin, or the first principle, of all that we experience. It deals with the non-phenomenal aspect of life. The word non-phenomenal refers to something that cannot be perceived through our five senses. Given this, metaphysics explains the appearance of that which is phenomenal, that which is perceivable by our five senses.

There is a metaphysical component to every aspect of our lives. The question is are we aware of it? Extra Sensory Perception (ESP) is a metaphysical topic that many in the scientific community do not take seriously. However, the concept of time is a subject of interest for both meta-physicists and physicists. Why is ESP not treated with the same level of interest as time is? It is because we all experience time, even though time is non-phenomenal. The same cannot be said of ESP. Many people do not believe in ESP or do not believe that they can perceive the extra sensory. What prevents us from experiencing the metaphysical is our beliefs.

The gulf between metaphysics and traditional science is beginning to narrow with the advent of quantum physics. Scientists are now discovering behaviors of the atomic world that go against everything we know in our physical world. Rather than choosing sides between the metaphysical and scientific, more and more researchers are incorporating both as they seek to find the answers to those larger questions that humanity has always pondered.

21 Metaphysical Secrets

The Nature of your Being and Existence

Do you exist? Anyone who is asked this question would give an instant and unqualified "yes!" How is it that we can answer this question without any sense of doubt? We can do so because we are aware of our existence. Because we are aware of our existence, we are also aware of the existence of all that we experience. How do you know you exist? What is your answer to this question? Regardless of what your answer is, you are aware of your answer as well! That aspect of you that is aware of your existence and your experiences is your being.

Throughout your life, you have had innumerable experiences, and all of them have involved change. You experienced change in your thoughts and beliefs. You have experienced change in your emotions and feelings. You have experienced change in your perceptions, and you have experienced change in your physical body. You have also experienced change in your surroundings. During the night, you experienced altered states of consciousness that gave rise to dreaming and deep sleep. You have experienced all of these changes; however, there is one constant. This constant has never changed. That constant is your awareness.

Everything that you experience occurs within the field of awareness, including that which you experience as being "you." That which we refer to as "awareness" is the fundamental nature of who you are.

Your being cannot be perceived through your senses or conceived by your mind; it can only be known intuitively. Anything that exists within awareness is what we refer to as experience. The existence of anything is the validation of the awareness of it. That which is aware is the nature of your being.

When speaking about consciousness, it easy to misinterpret what it is. No description will ever be given that captures the nature of consciousness because consciousness is beyond what the mind can understand. To help minimize the potential for confusion, let us replace the word "consciousness" with "knowing."

For knowing to exist, there needs to be three elements: The knower, the object that is known, and the knowing of the object. Let us use an example to illustrate this. I know that there is a tree in my yard. I (the knower) knows (the knowing of) there is a tree (the object).

Is it possible for me to separate the "knowing of" (also known as awareness) from the object of my awareness (the tree)? Determine this for yourself by looking at an object. Is the knowing of the object inseparable from the object itself? Of course, it is! The knowing of any object and the object that is known are inseparable from each other.

The knowing of your own existence is inseparable from existence itself. Thus,

your sense of self is an object of a greater knowing. Who or what has a knowing of you? Can you separate that which knows of you from the object that is you? That which knows of my own existence, can I separate it from the knowing that I have of the tree?

That which I refer to as "I," and my knowing of the tree, and the tree itself, are one in the same. That which knows of "I," and my knowing of the tree, and the tree itself, are also one in the same. Ultimately, all that there is knowing, or as I have used in this book, consciousness. You are an aspect of a greater consciousness.

For there to be a knowing of, there must be a knower and the object that is known. For pure consciousness to know anything, it must have an object to know. It is for this purpose that consciousness expresses itself in manifested from. You and I are an example of this manifestation.

For us to serve pure consciousness, it is necessary for us to take on physical form and a sense of individuality, or "I." It is this sense of "I," along with our identification with our physical form that creates a sense of separation from all the other forms of manifestation.

It is our sense of contrast between ourselves and other manifestations that creates new potentialities, which we know as thought. It is thought that creates our sense of experience and informs the pure or greater consciousness of its own nature. In response to our thoughts, the pure consciousness creates new potentialities that are consistent with the information that it has received from us.

What we refer to as consciousness is actually a consciousness system. You and I are localized aspects of the greater consciousness that are generating experiences for the larger consciousness system. Since we, localized consciousness, are inseparable from the greater consciousness, you and I are both the source of all of our experiences as well the experiencers of it. Our experience is what we refer to as existence, while the nature of being is that which knows of existence.

Do-It-Yourself Energy Experiment:

All of our problems, without exception, are the result of personalizing our experiences. We personalize our experiences because we identify with the thought that we have of our selves. By practice the exercise under the topic: Ego and Identity, you can recondition your mind to become an observer of your experiences, rather than personalizing them. The benefits of this will be greater peace, greater calm, expanded awareness, and diminishing judgmental thinking.

Nature of Reality: What is it?

In discussing *Existence and the Nature of Being,* we discussed that our essential being is awareness and that we know of existence because we are aware of it. Given the essential nature of our being is awareness, every living being is actually just one being.

If there is an awareness of that which you refer to as "you," and every other living being also has a sense of itself, then the essential aspect of all beings is the same awareness. Ultimately, all that there is awareness or consciousness. The nature of the world of form that we experience is the unlimited expressions of consciousness being projected through thought.

When dreaming, you experience yourself as a character that inhabits a dream world. This dream world seems so real that you do not realize it is just a dream until you wake up. Your dream self is fully engaged with its dream world. All of your senses are functioning. You can have thoughts, make plans, and take action.

As real as your dream experience may be, it is illusionary. Both your dream self and its dream world are the projections of your own consciousness. Just as you are the creator of your dream experience, universal consciousness expresses itself as individuated or localized forms of consciousness. These individuated expressions of consciousness experience themselves as being separate from the other localized expressions of consciousness. You and I are the localized expressions of the greater consciousness. Just as in the dream, we project our experiences which become our experience of reality.

There is no one objective reality; rather, each expression of consciousness is creating their own unique and subjective sense of reality, though there are some experiences that are part of the collective consciousness. It is for this reason that we all experience a "world" outside of ourselves; yet, that "world" will be experienced differently by each person.

Do-It-Yourself Energy Experiment:

Practice suspending judgment and the need to be right. Also, practice letting go of the need to be certain about what things mean. Doing both of these things will allow you to experience going beyond your sense of certainty and experience a perspective that you may have never experienced before. It will increase your sense of creativity and compassion.

The Things that We do: Determinism versus Free Will

What is the origin of your behaviors? Do you freely choose your behaviors, or are your behaviors the results of factors outside of yourself? Determinism is the school of thought that governs most of the sciences and many schools of psychology. An example would be B. F. Skinner who conditioned a dog to salivate after repeatedly presenting a piece of meat while ringing a bell at the same time. Before the dog learned to associate the meat with the bell, it would salivate just by seeing the meat. After the dog learned to associate the sound of the bell with the meat, it salivated just from hearing the sound of the bell.

Imagine that you are on the freeway driving over the speed limit, until you see a police car following you. The sight of the police car causes you to adjust your speed. The salivating of the dog and the adjustment of your speed were both the effects of environmental factors, namely the bell and the police officer.

As opposed to determinism, the concept of free will states that our behaviors are a product of our free choice, that we choose our behavior rather than our behavior being the result of some environmental factor.

The challenge posed by the concepts of determinism and free will is that they are both the product of our rational mind. The mind is only able to understand the phenomenal world, meaning that which can be detected by the senses or through the experience of thought. The mind is unable to detect the non-phenomenal. How we perceive that which we refer to as the self can make a big difference as to whether we see our actions as being the result of external factors or from free will.

If we see ourselves as being a distinct, physical entity that lives in a world populated by objects and other physical beings, then determinism would seem to make sense. By seeing ourselves as distinct, physical entities, everything that we experience will be perceived as being separate from ourselves. I see the furniture in my home or my family members as being separate entities from myself because I see myself as a separate being unto myself. It would make sense that my behaviors are the result of my interactions with these and other entities. An argument could also be made that some of my behaviors can also spring from free choice. My wife may ask me to do a certain task. My handling the task for her would seem to fit the model of determinism. However, I have the free will to schedule my doing of the task when it would work best for both of us. So, is my behavior a product of determinism, free-will, or both?

Do you have control of your thoughts? How long can you go without having a thought? Do you have control over the sensations that you experience? Can you control the rate at which your body ages? Can you control the flow of your blood or the metabolism of your body? The deeper that we look into our lives, the more that we see that so much of our life is not in our control. We cannot control our dreams, nor can we control the length of our life span.

If you have ever practiced meditation at a deep enough level, it is indisputable that we have an awareness of all of our experiences. We experience the world through the five senses, and we have an awareness of our perceptions, our sensations, the sounds that we hear, and that which we taste. If we are aware of all of these forms of sensory input, then we cannot be our experiences, including our experience of the body and thought.

As we are aware of the physical body and our mental functions, who we are, at the deepest level, cannot be the physical body or our mental functions. That which is awareness, is it subject to determinism or free will? How can awareness be subject to determinism or free will when all of experience is dependent on the awareness of it? Awareness is ever present. Whether we are wide awake, dreaming, or in a deep sleep, there is an awareness of it. Determinism and free will can only exist if there is an awareness of it.

If we see ourselves as a multidimensional being, that we are both phenomenal and non-phenomenal in nature, perhaps we can agree on one thing, we have the free-will to direct our focus and attention. Ultimately, that may be the only thing that we are in control of.

Mind and Matter: Does it Matter?

In western society, we have been socialized to believe that the world is divided into an inner and the outer realms. We directly experience our thoughts, perceptions, and sensation, all of which we refer to as aspects of ourselves. These things are considered to be our inner realm. The objects of our thoughts, perceptions, and sensations are experienced as our outer realm.

We experience the world through our five senses and make sense of it through our thoughts. We equate our thoughts to the "mind." No one has ever seen a "mind," though we have been socialized to believe that we have one. On the other hand, everything that we experience with our five senses can be known as it has a physical reality to it. It can be measured, weighed, touched, and so on. It is from this separation of these two realms that we come up with concepts such as "mind over matter" or "mind and matter."

The divide between mind and matter is an illusion, an illusion created by thought. The reason why the ancient practice of meditation remains thriving today is that the illusion of separation between mind and body cannot hold up to deeper inspection.

Try this simple experiment. If you are experienced in meditation, get into a relaxed meditative state. If you are inexperienced in meditation, simply close your eyes and relax. Avoid engaging with your thoughts by simply accepting everything that you experience without judgment or trying to control anything.

As the activity of your mind starts to slow down, place your attention on your thoughts. That you can pay attention to your thoughts demonstrates that your thoughts can be perceived by you; you have a knowing of their existence. Now place your attention on the chair or the floor that you are sitting on. You are aware of the sensations that arise from that which you are sitting on it.

The chair or the floor that you are sitting on, according to our socialization and conditioning, is made of matter. As you experience sensations of the surface that you are sitting on, you experience it as being something outside of yourself (unlike thought). Also, the surface that you are sitting on has volume and mass (unlike thought). Both thought and the surface that you are sitting on are recognized by you through awareness. You are aware of the movement of thought, and you are aware of the sensations of the surface.

Now go back into your meditation and determine for yourself as to whether you can separate your awareness of thought from the thought itself. Can you separate the awareness of the sensation of the surface from the surface itself?

The awareness of anything is inseparable from that which you are aware of. How can mind and matter be separate when both thought and the surface are inseparable from awareness?

Mind and matter are but properties of our conceptual thinking. It is our limited perception that leads us to believe that they are of separate realities.

Do-It-Yourself Energy Experiment:

Practice the exercise, described in this topic, until you experience yourself as no longer begin separate from the world around you. You will know that you have reached this level of awareness when your experience of yourself seems to merge with that which you are observing, which is the essence of love. The benefits of this exercise are that you will recondition your mind so that your sense of connection with life will be enhanced.

What is the Universe?

Under the topic of *Mind and Matter*, you were guided to the discovery that mind and matter are not separate, that they are both manifestations of consciousness. Anything that we attribute to being an aspect of the mind or matter is also a manifestation of consciousness. Given this, even your sense of self and your physical body is a manifestation as well. The universe that we experience is not something that exists outside of us. Rather, the universe that we experience is a manifestation of consciousness and is projected from within us.

The Law of Attraction has received much attention since the release of the 2006 bestseller, the *Secret*. The theme of the book is that you manifest your world and that you can attract that which you desire with your thoughts. Whether you believe in the Law of Attraction or not is irrelevant when viewed from the perspective of higher awareness. The reason for this is that everyone is attracting their experiences of life, whether they are conscious of it or not. After all, the essence of who we are is inseparable from the rest of life. If you believe in the Law of Attraction and are practicing it, then you are consciously manifesting in your life as opposed to manifesting unconsciously. This is the only difference between believing in the Law of Attraction and not believing in it.

The Nature of Happiness: An Endless Search

Like everything else in life, how we experience happiness is dependent upon our level of conscious awareness. For most of humanity, happiness is experienced as an emotion when an unfulfilled desire is met. A person who is unhappy because they feel lonely may become happy upon starting a relationship with someone new. Similarly, a person may be struggling financially and then become happy upon receiving a large sum of money. In either case, the happiness that is experienced is contingent upon the circumstances of the person aligning with their desires.

When the person's circumstances do not align with their desires, their happiness will fade. The person who found a new relationship may later get their feelings hurt by the other person. The person who received a large sum of money may discover that they are responsible for paying a large tax bill.

Because happiness, for most of us, is based on external conditions, our happiness is transitory.

For others, especially, in the spiritual community, happiness is sought not in their external conditions but from within. Perhaps they believe in God, or some universal power. Because their focus is not on external conditions, their sense of happiness may seem more stable. However, even this experience of happiness has its pitfalls.

When people who are following a spiritual path feel happy, they reinforce the belief that it is their spiritual path that is making them happy. However, there will be times when they feel unhappy. At such times, they may resist the feelings of unhappiness because they may feel that they should not feel that way. This resistance to experiencing unhappiness can lead to the person either blocking out their feelings or engage in self-doubt. There is another alternative, which is the understanding that happiness is something that cannot be pursued or gained. The nature of happiness is such that it arises when we stop searching for it.

There is an inherent peace that lies within the depths of us all. Its existence is independent of anything outside of us or any spiritual path. To unveil and realize this inner peace only requires inquiry into one's self.

When we establish our lives in this place, we can experience any emotion yet remain untouched by it. Whether it is the emotion of ecstasy or grief, the emotion is fully experienced; yet, a sense of peace and acceptance underlies it all. It is like a person who is watching a movie. During the movie, there may be scenes of sadness, conflict, hope, and victory. While the person may be caught up in the movie, he or she knows that it is just a movie.

When we establish inner peace within us, there is nothing that we can experience that will rob us of our peace, which cannot be said of happiness. How do we learn to establish inner peace? It is actually very simple. It is simple because there is nothing for us to establish! It is the very nature of our existence to be at peace. The reason why we do not experience peace is not because we have to gain anything; rather, we need to lose something. That something is our self-identification with our mind. The essence of who we are is the knower of thoughts, emotions, feelings, perceptions, and sensations. When we learn to observe them, without getting involved with them, we will reconnect with our sense of peace.

Do-It-Yourself Energy Experiment:

Learning to meditate is a great way to connect with the sense of peace described in this topic. Most meditations that are taught ask you to visualize a peaceful scene or to focus on something, like your breath. Instead, try meditating but do not focus on anything. Do not visualize or try to control anything. Allow yourself to experience whatever you are experiencing without trying to get involved with it. To quote a Beetles tune, "Let it Be."

Does Time Exist?

Time is just an illusion. We experience linear time and believe it to be real. Einstein showed that time is relative and is part of a time-space continuum. Past and future are illusionary. Everything that has ever existed, or will exist, exists in the present. It is our mind that creates a sense of past and future. Our conditioning and beliefs affect our experience of time. The less we cling to our conditioning and beliefs, the more we will experience timelessness.

Our experience of time and space is based on our identifying with body and mind. We believe that the thoughts that we experience are our thoughts. We believe that the emotions and feelings that we experience are our emotions and feelings. We believe the body that we experience is our body. Anything that we experience that is apart from our minds and bodies is experience as being something separate from ourselves. Our sense of time and space is based on this sense of separation.

The deepest level of consciousness is pure consciousness, which is devoid of all thought or memory. The qualities of pure consciousness are oneness, wholeness, boundless, and eternal. Everything that exists, phenomenal or non-phenomenal, arises from pure consciousness; however, it is not separate from pure consciousness. To illustrate this, imagine a drop from the ocean. The drop is an expression of the ocean that has qualities that are vastly different from the ocean. The drop is of much smaller size, lacks the waves and currents of the ocean, nor does it harbor the abundance of marine life that the ocean does. However, its essential composition is no different than the ocean. The drop contains the same chemical composition as the ocean itself. If you return the drop to the ocean, it merges with it without any distinction.

Thought is a manifestation of pure consciousness. As with the drop and the ocean, thought has many qualities that are unique, but its essential nature is the same as pure consciousness. Unlike pure consciousness, thoughts can be perceived by our awareness. We know when we are experiencing a thought. Thoughts contain information (which we refer to as memory), while pure consciousness is devoid of information. Finally, thoughts are fleeting in their existence, unlike pure consciousness which is eternally present. Despite all these differences, the essential nature of thought is pure consciousness. Everything that we experience is pure consciousness appearing in an infinite variety of forms.

Thought is like a filter through which pure consciousness is converted into what we refer to as time and space. At the level of pure consciousness, time, distance, space, separation, variety, distinctions, boundaries, and limitations are non-existent. Thought is like a snap shot of pure consciousness while at the same time creating the impression of qualities that we experience as reality. Among those qualities are time and space.

There is no such thing as time and space. Time and space are the constructions of the mind that are projected on to our experience of reality. These constructs of the mind are like an image projected on a screen. The images of the movie comes from the projector and are projected on screen. If you turn off the projector, the screen would become blank. Similarly, if we let go of our attachment to our thoughts, we would not project them on that which we are experiencing.

What we experience as being time is the movement of thought. We may have one thought that tells us that the candle on our table is burning. Later, we may have the thought that the candle has burned down to half of its original size. We experience these changes as the passing of time. In fact, everything that has ever existed is occurring at the same time.

We will discuss this in more detail under the topic of parallel universes.

Do-It-Yourself Energy Experiment:

You can change your experience of time if you learn to divert your attention away from your thoughts. Next time you do something that you enjoy, notice how the passage of time differs from when you are doing something that you do not enjoy. Normally, your experience of time speeds up when you are doing something you enjoy because you are more engaged with the task at hand. When doing a task that you do not enjoy, the passage of time tends to be slower because you are spending more time paying attention to your thoughts.

Does God Exist?

The truth of God cannot be experienced through the mind, nor can it be experienced through religion or some sacred texts. Even prayer, in most cases, is not directed toward God's truth. The reason for this is that any concept that we have of God is just that, a concept. A concept is a form of thought. How can a thought of "God" know the truth of God's existence? A thought cannot know anything; thought is just information. The awareness that knows of the existence of thought is more primal greater than thought itself.

By its very nature, the rational mind cannot conceive that which is non-phenomenal. Our minds can only detect the phenomenal, meaning that which we can perceive through our five senses and experience as thought. For most of humanity, the experience of God is contained within our thoughts, perceptions, feelings, or feelings. How else can we experience God? The challenge is that most of humanity identifies themselves with their mind and body. Any quality or characteristic that we give to our experience of God is the result of our own minds, not through the knowing of God.

As we discussed throughout this book, your fundamental nature is awareness or consciousness. Anything that you will ever experience is an object in the field of your awareness. The truth of who you are, the source of awareness, cannot be known by your conscious mind. The closest you will ever come to knowing your true self, in this lifetime, is in deep sleep. As stated earlier, deep sleep is devoid of thought and experience. We have no memory of deep sleep; yet, we are aware of the fact that it occurred. There could be no existence if there was no awareness of it. Pure consciousness, God, and your essential nature are one in the same.

The perspective that most of humanity holds is that we are a physical being that has a mind, from which thinking occurs. Because we experience ourselves as physical beings, we experience a sense of separation. As individual beings, we see ourselves as beings that are separate entities from all other physical forms. It is this sense of separation that creates our experience of time. It is our fixation on the world of form, along with illusions of time that leads us to believe that there is only one reality, the reality that we experience.

When viewed from the perspective of higher consciousness, that which we call reality is illusionary. From this perspective, time and separation do not exist. From this perspective, there are innumerable realities that are occurring all at the same time. To understand this, we first need to take a deeper look at the nature of energy and thought.

The fundamental ingredient of that which we refer to as the universe is energy and information. Everything that exists is made of energy, which has an innate intelligence to it. It is this intelligence that allows energy to take on multiple forms, which can be exemplified by the different phases that water can take on. Water can appear as a gas, liquid, or solid. What triggers a change in the phase that water takes on is temperature. The higher the temperature, the further apart are its water molecules. The lower the temperature, the closer the water molecules are to each other.

Molecules are composed of atoms, and over 90% of what constitutes an atom is energy. It is the information contained in energy that allows water to express itself in its various potentials. As time does not exist, other than a concept within our mind, all potentials exist at the same moment. Meaning, the potentials for water to be a liquid, solid, or gas can all exist at the same time. Given that we only experience one dimension of reality, it appears that the passage of time is required for water to change into its different phases.

It is only our conceptual mind that makes it appear that our experience of reality is the only reality. By learning to develop higher states of awareness, there is an infinite number of realities that we can experience. In our current reality, you are your current age. In another reality, you may be dead, while in another reality you have yet to be born.

The nature of reality is determined by our identification with thought. The less we cling to any given thought, the more open we will become to experience other realities or universes.

It is only at the level of ordinary awareness that we experience birth and death. As our fundamental nature is consciousness, our lives are eternal. The physical body is just an expression of consciousness, not the essence of who we are.

Everything in this life undergoes entropy, where the atomic particles of an object fluctuate between randomness and order. A metaphor for entropy would be the way water takes on different states. In its liquid form, water molecules have a lot of space between them, allowing them to move freely. This freedom of movement is why liquids can take on the shape of the space that it occupies. When water freezes, it becomes a solid, which we refer to as ice.

As ice, the water molecules are in direct contact with each other, offering little room for movement. When water is boiled, or evaporates, it becomes a gas. In its gas form, the water molecules have vast distances between them. Because of this, water loses all appearance of form or physicality.

In its solid state, the molecules have an order to them, while there is randomness in its gaseous state.

The water molecules themselves are composed of atoms, two hydrogen atoms, and one oxygen atom. While the atom was once considered a solid particle, we now know that this is just an illusion. The atom is actually made of subatomic particles separated from each other by vast distances of space. Even the subatomic particles lack any solidity to them as they are actually fluctuations of energy.

What we know as to be water is, at its most fundamental level, energy that takes on different configurations that result in it taking on different appearances, according to our perception.

We are no different than water in that we are also composed of atoms and molecules. Just as water takes on different states, we too take on different forms. Birth and death are the names that we have given to our experience of entropy. At the most fundamental level, there is no distinction between you, me, and this book that you are reading. Reincarnation is the name that we have given to the changing of entropy.

Most of us consider Extra Sensory Perception to be a special gift if we believe in it at all. One reason for this is the result of how we perceive ourselves and thought. We experience ourselves as distinct entities onto ourselves, separate from other people. We also believe that our thoughts are generated from our brains and that they are uniquely our own. As we ascend to higher level of consciousness, we begin to realize that any sense of separation is just an illusion. As for the origin of thoughts, how can we have our own thoughts when our sense of separation is just an illusion?

Thoughts are not generated by your mind; rather, you attract thoughts to you, which you experience as being yours.

Each one of us has the potential to experience any thought that has ever or will ever exist. The ability to tap into higher levels of consciousness is what we refer to as ESP, and any one of us can do it. What prevents some of us from realizing our ESP abilities are the beliefs that we hold on to. The following are examples of beliefs that prevent us from tapping into our ability for ESP:

- ESP is not real.
- I don't have ESP.
- ESP is a special ability.

Just as with experiencing parallel universes, the less that we identify with our thoughts, the greater we will be able to experience ESP.

The Awareness of Awareness: How Deep Can you Go?

Take a moment to look at your surroundings. Now place your attention on yourself. Having done so, answer these two questions: Are you are aware of your surroundings? Are you aware of yourself? The answer to both of these questions would be an immediate "yes"! Additionally, you are aware of thought, of the images that appear in your mind, and the sensations that you feel. Here is another question. Do you exist? The answer to that question would be another resounding "yes." You are aware of all of these things, but there is a more subtle level of awareness that you may not have ever considered: Are you aware of being aware?

Nothing can be experienced unless there is an awareness of it, even the most profound and subtlest forms of experience are detected by our awareness. Experience owes its existence to awareness.

When sleeping, we go through different levels of sleep. At the first level of sleep, we redirect our attention from the outer world and focus on the internal world. At this stage, we still have a strong identification with our physical body and mind. In the dream state, our sense of identification with the body greatly diminishes, and our awareness is heightened, allowing us to experience our subconscious thoughts and memories. We call these subconscious thoughts and memories "dreams." In deep sleep, we lose all sense of identification with our physical body and mind as our awareness retreats further within.

In deep sleep, we return to the source of awareness itself, pure consciousness. Pure consciousness is devoid of all thoughts or memory. It is for this reason that you are unable to remember your experience of deep sleep. For there to be an experience, there must be a memory of it. There can be no memory without thought, which is why we are unable to recall our experience of deep sleep. Despite this fact, we know that we experienced deep sleep. How can that be? While we have no memory of deep sleep, we still had an awareness of it. You have an awareness of that which is beyond thought or memory! The reason why you have an awareness of deep sleep is because who you are at the most fundamental level is awareness itself. At your most essential form, you are the awareness of deep sleep, dreams, your mind, your physical body, and everything else that you experience. You are awareness that is aware of itself.

What is your Purpose?

As long as we experience ourselves as purely physical beings separate from the rest of life, we will feel the need for a sense of purpose. The need for a sense of purpose is real and having a sense of purpose can powerfully impact our lives. On the other hand, having a lack of purpose can also lead to a sense of being disconnected from others and feeling that our lives have no meaning.

The idea of a life purpose is the sole property of the mind. Nowhere but in the human species does the purpose of life become an issue. Nature functions beautifully without pondering life's purpose.

The greater we elevate our consciousness awareness, the less necessary a life's purpose will be needed. Consider the state of deep sleep. Who among us does not enjoy the experience of waking up in the morning after spending the night in deep sleep? During deep sleep, did you worry about your purpose in life? Yet, you woke up feeling fresh and renewed. The need for a purpose in life is the product of the ego. This is not to say that having a sense of purpose is not necessary; it is as long as we are controlled by the ego. The key thing to ask one's self is "Am I happy?" If not having a sense of purpose is making you unhappy, then it may be something that is worthwhile to explore. If you can be happy without a sense of purpose, a sense of purpose is not needed.

When pursuing one's life purpose, three misunderstandings make it difficult to identify one's life purpose. The first misunderstanding is that one's life purpose must be something of grand scale or that it will impact the world. In truth, one's life purpose could be as simple being a better parent or doing volunteer work in the community. To better understand this, if a person's search for life's purpose is driven by the ego, that person is really being driven by the need to feel significant. Such a person will focus on those things that will be more grandiose and which will put them in the spotlight.

In contrast, consider someone who gets involved doing volunteer work in their community out of the desire to contribute. Because they enjoy what they are doing, they will more likely be led to their life purpose.

The main thing is not to spend time pondering your life purpose; rather, expose yourself to new situations and be aware of those situations that resonate with you. Your feelings for a situation are more reliable in identifying your life's purpose than is your rational thinking.

Do-It-Yourself Energy Experiment:

The following are guidelines for finding your purpose:

1. Stop thinking about your life's purpose and start exposing yourself to new experiences. That which resonates with you will align with your purpose.

2. Make a list of all the things that you enjoy doing.

3. Make a list of all of your strengths and abilities.

4. Identify a need that others have.

5. Determine how you could apply steps 2 and 3 to fulfill the need in step 4.

As discussed in the topic on reincarnation, the essence of your life is eternal. As a species that is deeply attached to our conceptual thinking, we experience birth and death as the expression of new life and the loss of existing life. From the perspective of higher awareness, there is no new life or loss of existing life; there is only life. What we refer to as life and death are just two sides of the same coin. Birth and death are our perceptions and conceptual understandings of an eternal life force that is constantly creating new configurations of expression.

The Experience of Experience

You experience things, but who or what is experiencing you? And that which experiences you, can it be experienced? Here is a simple exercise for inquiring on the nature of you.

1. Take a moment to relax and then look around your surroundings.
2. Pick an object in your environment and place your attention on it.

Now that you have done this, I have a question for you: What was the object that you were looking at? However you answer this question, your answer was formulated as a thought. If your answer to this question was that you were observing a tree, that answer was experienced as a thought. If you were observing a tree, then that was a perception. You had a perception and a thought of a tree.

My next question for you is how do you know that you had a perception and a thought of a tree? You knew you had a perception and a thought because there was awareness of it. There can be no experience without the awareness of it. Both "thought," "perception," and "tree" are concepts that we learned about when we were young. We can never know anything about "thought," "perception," or "tree." Can you touch, feel, measure, or observe a concept? Of course, you can't. We can only know the existence of them.

As you grew up, you learned about different concepts, and you started associating them to your experience. As a certain age, you replaced your pure experience of the world with concepts of it. As an infant, my experience of a tree was pure, unfiltered by the concepts that I had yet to learn. That changed when I started gaining information from those around me. Anything that I learned about trees, from that point on, became another concept that was combined with the existing concepts that I had of trees.

Today, I can name different species of trees. I can tell you of their size, their color, or their shape. Concepts are useful when communicating information about trees, but they can never take the place of the tree. Concepts are just a form of thought. I can think of a "tree"; I can hold concepts of a "tree," and I can perceive a "tree," but none of these are the tree itself

My thoughts and perceptions of a "tree" are like the experiences of the blind men and the elephant. Just as they never could experience the truth of the elephant, my thoughts and perceptions can never know the truth of a tree. All that I can ever know of a tree are my thoughts and perceptions of it. This is not just true of the tree; it is true for all of experience.

We can never know anything about our experiences other than our awareness of them. Any meaning we give to our experiences is a product of our thoughts. That which we experience has no inherent meaning; we create the meaning of our experiences. Who you are at your most essential level is the one who creates experiences and gives meaning to it; yet, your essential being is untouched by any experience. A light that shines on water illuminates the water; however, the light never becomes wet. You are the awareness of all experience, yet no experience can touch awareness.

Do-It-Yourself Energy Experiment:

Learning to not hold on to your conceptual thinking is a great way to experience expanded awareness. While concepts come in handy when communicating information, clinging to them create boundaries to our ability to experience. The reason for this is that we are focusing on our concepts, which prevent us from considering what lies beyond them. Besides meditation, the following is another way to practice perceiving without resorting to concepts:

1. Sit down and make yourself comfortable.

2. Take a few minutes to scan your environment, observing the people, plants, animals, or objects that are within your vicinity.

3. Now close your eyes and imagine that you are from another planet and have been sent to planet Earth to gather information about it. Being that you are from outer space, you have no previous knowledge or experience of Earth. You are like a newborn baby seeing the world for the first time.

4. Now open your eyes and look around again as you did the first time, remembering not to interpret, label, or judge anything that you see. Observe as though you were a blank slate.

Did your second observation have a different quality to it as compared to your first observation? Many people report that their second observation seemed fresh and more vibrant, that they felt more connected to life and themselves, that they felt more peaceful. If you were unable to detect a difference between the two observations, continue to practice until you can discern a difference.

Thoughts and Beliefs: The Creation of Meaning

As discussed previously in this book, we do not have thoughts; we do not generate thoughts from our brain. In other words, your thoughts are not yours! We have been socialized to believe that our thoughts belong to us because we have developed a deep identification with mind and body. In fact, there is no such thing as a "mind." What we refer to as "mind" is just a thought.

We previously discussed that deep sleep is devoid of thought as deep sleep is really the experience of pure consciousness. What we refer to as thought is a manifestation of the pure consciousness. There are various gradations of manifestation of the pure consciousness. The manifestations of consciousness appear in gradations of physicality. At one end of the spectrum are those things that we know as light and thought. Both light and thought have no physicality about them. On the other end of the spectrum are those things that we perceive to have physicality such as our bodies. In truth, non-physicality and physicality are just qualities of our perceptions rather than being the inherent quality of the manifestation.

As previously stated, the human body is perceived as being a physical structure but is, in fact, devoid of physicality at the atomic level. If you and I lack physicality, where does the sense of "I" come from? We live our entire lives referring to "I" or variations of it, such as "my" "mine," or "me." What is this "I?"

Your sense of "I" is just a thought. You have an awareness of your own existence. The thought "I" is the recognition of our own existence. The thought "I" is the like a name tag that is worn by awareness. However, this thought is not awareness. Rather, you are aware of it. It is like having a thought of a car. The thought of a car is not the car; it just references it.

When your sense of "I" interacts with its other manifestations, it experiences contrast. To illustrate this, let us use a small child as an example. A child knows that it exists; he or she has an awareness of its own existence. The child is given two items of food to choose from them. The first item is a piece of candy and the second item is spinach. By sampling each of the food items, the child can experience contrast: The two items of food taste different from each other. This experience of contrast is what we know as experience.

The child's thought of "I" identifies with the experience of tasting the foods. For example, the "I" thought may identify with the thought "candy is more pleasurable than spinach." The "I" thought becomes a magnet that attracts other thoughts that are of the same quality. For example, the thought "I prefer candy" will attract other thoughts that are of similar quality such as "I want something sweet" or "Foods that are brightly colored are good."

Where do the thoughts that are attracted to the "I" thought come from? They come from what we sometimes refer to as the collective consciousness. Every thought that has ever been thought, or will be thought, exist already with the collective consciousness, also known as the Akashi Records. This is why it was stated earlier that you do not create or own your thoughts; rather, your "I" thought attracts them to it. The thought that is attracted are those thoughts that match the quality of thoughts that you have previously attracted. The child who had the thought "I like candy" will attract other thoughts that are consistent with that thought.

No thought has inherent power of its own. Any power that a thought possess is derived from the attention that we give it. If we remove our attention from a thought, it will lose its potency. When we give a great amount of attention to a thought, that thought becomes a belief. A belief is very powerful because it becomes a filter to how we experience life. If a person develops the belief that people cannot be trusted, that person will experience every interaction that they have as something they need to be suspect of. When we give a great deal of our attention to a belief, it becomes a conviction. Our convictions are so powerful that some people will kill themselves or others because of it.

Do-It-Yourself Energy Experiment:

The reason why the practice of meditation has to withstand the test of time is because it addresses a timeless problem, getting caught up in our thoughts. As stated before, the meaning of our experiences is not inherent in the experience. Instead, all meaning comes from the thoughts that we have of our experience. The practice of meditation and non-judgment are effective ways for reconditioning our mind. For most of us, our socialization has taught us to identify with our thoughts. Mediation and non-judgment train our attention so that we can be aware of our thoughts but not get involved with them.

The following exercise can be used to discover your core beliefs. Discovering your core beliefs is fundamental to making changes in your life.

1. The first step is to think of an ongoing challenge that you are experiencing in your life. My example will be: I am afraid of public speaking.
2. My next step is to start a line of inquiry using the phrase "What would be so bad if..." So my first question would be "What would be so bad about public speaking?"

3. My answer to that question would be "I might make a mistake or get nervous."

4. I would then use my response and rephrase the question: "What would be so bad if I made a mistake or was nervous?"

5. My response to that would be "People would think less of me."

6. I would continue to repeat this question by asking: "What would be so bad if people felt less of me?"
   My answer to that would be "I would feel like I am unlovable."

7. Keep going through this line of questioning until you are unable to any further. When you have reached this point, you will have identified your subconscious belief. At the conscious level, I am aware of the fear of public speaking; however, the core belief behind that belief is "I feel like I am unlovable."

That which lies beyond Ego and Personal Identity

In the previous topic, we explored thoughts and beliefs. At your purest essence, you are devoid of a sense of ego or personal identity. That which we refer to as ego and personal identity are also thoughts and perceptions that we have of ourselves. Both ego and personality are like garments that your essential truth wears to experience the world. If you had no sense of "I," you could not have any sense of experience.

Ego is just a form of thought; however, it is the most powerful thought that we have regarding our level of conviction that we have for it. Your sense of identity is just a belief system. If you change your beliefs about yourself, you can change your identity. By learning how to create distance between yourself and your thoughts, you can reconfigure your mind so that you diminish our sense of identification with the ego and your sense of identity.

The following are some simple exercises, which with practice, can lead you to challenge your perceptions of who you are. Note: These exercises need to be continuously practiced to break through your conditioning and the belief systems that you have of yourself. The purpose of this exercise is to challenge your beliefs as to the nature of that which you refer to as "I."

1. Sit down, make yourself comfortable, and closed eyes.
2. Place your focus on your breathing.
3. When you feel relaxed, take note of any thoughts that you may be having. You can take note of thoughts because you are aware of them.
4. Now try to locate the "you" that is aware of thought. The "you" that I am referring to is that which each one of us calls "I."

73

Where is this "I" located, the one that is aware of thought? What are the qualities of this "I"? Is it big? Is it small? Does it have a color? Regardless of how you respond to these questions, you have not discovered the truth of who you are. Everything that you experience, including the answers to these questions, is also observed. Who you are at your most essential level cannot be experienced by you. That which you refer to as "I" is just another object being observed within your awareness. That which you refer to as "I" is a thought that you have learned to identify with. Who you are is that which observes all of experience!

Your sense of identity is just a set of beliefs that you have adopted for you to fit in with your family, culture, or society that you found yourself in.

As consciousness, you are the observer of all of experience, including your sense of "I" and your sense of identity.

Do-It-Yourself Energy Experiment:

The exercise described under this topic allows you to experience the letting go of your identification with your mind and body. It does take persistent practice, but the benefits are innumerable, including:

- Spending less time thinking and more time experiencing life.
- Developing a greater sense of connection with others.
- Transcending any critical thinking that you may have of yourself and others.
- Staying present
- Becoming more open to experience
- Transcending fears.
- Overcoming addictive behaviors.

Like everything else that we experience as being part of "reality," the subject of cause and effect is relative toward the level of awareness that it is being experienced from. Our everyday experience is found in the third-dimensional reality (the reality of physical form). It is in this reality that we can predict causation. If I throw a baseball at a window, the glass breaks. If I throw a ball up in the air, it will fall back to Earth. If I don't go to work, I will get fired. Most of what we understand of cause and effect is the result of Newtonian physics. Newtonian physics explains the laws that govern our world through the relationships between the motion of objects and the forces acting upon them. Much of our traditional scientific understanding came from Newtonian physics.

The advent of quantum physics shook the very foundation of Newtonian physics. At the atomic level, the ability to predict cause with effect was smashed. Researchers found solid particles acting like waves and waves acting like solid particles. They discovered that two particles could occupy the same space at the same time. They found that it is impossible to measure the velocity and direction of an atomic particle at the same time. In short, everything that we experience with a sense of certainty in our daily reality was lost at the quantum level.

Under the topic *That which lies beyond Ego and Personal Identity,* it was explained that which we refer to as "I" is just a thought of which we have identified with. How can we be sure that we know the correct relationship between cause and effect when most of the human species confuse the "I" thought with who they are? It is possible that which we take to be cause and effect is just our own dogmatic interpretation of what is really correlation?

Many religions have used cause and effect, known as karma, to maintain societal obedience. According to some religions, living in poverty is the result of past karma and that to change one's karma takes many life times. To have an impoverished population believe this makes it that much easier for the ruling party to maintain civil obedience.

Let's look at a different perspective of karma, as it relates to cause and effect. Every moment is a karmic moment, and every karmic moment lasts only as long as we allow it to. To better understand this, let us first look at the karmic cycle. The karmic cycle includes memory, desire, and action.

Let us say that you are walking on the street and you pass a restaurant. You detect a most pleasurable smell coming from it. The reason that you can identify that smell is because you have a memory of it from the past. The memory of the smell elicits the desire to taste the food. Your desire causes you to enter the restaurant and order the food, which is the action component of the karmic cycle. Once you have taken action by eating the food, you have completed the karmic cycle. The action of eating the food reinforces the existing memory of it, and the cycle continues.

Now let us look at a different scenario. Let us say that you are walking down the same street, and you smell the food coming from the restaurant. Instead of entering the restaurant, you walk past the restaurant. By walking past the food, you have changed your karma. The karmic cycle has been completed; however, your actions have created a new memory. The creation of a new memory creates a new desire and a new future.

If you look into last two scenarios more deeply, you may realize two important points. The first point is that karma can be changed in a moment. The second point is that your experience of karma had nothing to do with restaurant. In other words, it is not the circumstances in your life that influence your karma; rather, it is how you respond to them that determines it.

The most powerful thing that we can do to improve the quality of our lives is to develop greater awareness to the choices that we are making on a moment to moment basis. When we become conscious of our decision making, we become a conscious participant to the workings of the entire universe. When we become conscious decision makers, we enhance the quality of our lives and of all those around us.

What is Freedom?

Freedom is a universally desired by all living beings. Everyone wants to live a life free from restrictions or unpleasant conditions. The challenge for most of humanity is that the pursuit of freedom has its focus on the external world while ignoring the inner world. Imagine a person who is experiencing financial distress and is struggling just to make ends meet. This person does not experience the feeling of freedom because they are focusing on all the lack that exists in their lives.

Now suppose that this person's financial situation changes for the better. They start a business that becomes very successful, and they enjoy a dramatic change in income. This person now experiences numerous opportunities to enjoy themselves because of their success, which was nonexistent in the past. This person now enjoys a sense of freedom that they never had before.

While this person is enjoying their new life, they discover that a dear friend or family member has been diagnosed with cancer or some other life threatening disease. All of the sudden, the sense of freedom that this person was enjoying evaporates from their lives.

Because of our socialization and conditioning, we have come to be stimulus-response beings whose sense of freedom is dependent upon on whether or not the conditions of our life are aligned with our expectations. When the conditions of our life are aligned with our deepest desires, we experience a sense of freedom. However, this sense of freedom is impermanent. The nature of life is constant change. Any sense of freedom will last only as long as our conditions remain unchanged.

For most people, a sense of freedom comes about when they can escape from a situation that they find aversive. True freedom arises when we can experience a sense of peace regardless of the conditions that we experience.

Regardless of what we experience, no experience can enslave us or take away our freedom. From the perspective of higher consciousness, all of experience is ultimately a projection of pure consciousness. Everything that we experience, including our sense of being a person, and the thought of freedom, is just a potentiality that is being expressed by the greater consciousness.

Duality and Non-Duality: The Oneness of Many

.

The term "duality" means "two," while the term "non-duality" means "not two." The human species overwhelmingly experiences life from a dualistic perspective. "Us and them," "mine and yours," "good and bad," and "big and small," are all examples of dualism.

For most of the scientific age, the mind was viewed as separate from the body. It was only toward the modern age of science that the separation between mind and body began to dissolve. Research demonstrated that activity in the brain can affect the body, while activity in the body can affect the mind. At the same time, it is normal for people to experience the activity and functions of the mind as being separate from those of the body.

If you are worried our making your mortgage payment, most likely you are not giving thought to your body. If you just broke your arm, you most likely will not give attention to thoughts as they arise and fade in your consciousness. Both of these examples are legitimate perspectives of the mind-body relationship. To say that mind and body are separate from each other is a dualistic perspective. By saying that the mind body relationship is neither separate nor one is a nondual perspective.

The problems caused by concepts, as we discussed previously, extend to teachings of non-duality. Many teachers of non-duality treat it as something separate from duality, which is a dualistic perspective. A deeper look reveals that duality is found in non-duality and non-duality is found in duality.

While pure consciousness is one, its manifested expressions are infinite in their variety. Everything that we experience is a manifestation of pure consciousness. As limitless are the manifestations of pure consciousness are, every manifestation is pure consciousness at its most fundamental level. We can illustrate this by using a television set. Digital waves are filled with information that has been broken down. These waves are picked-up by the television, and their information is unscrambled. The image that we see on the television screen is formed by the numerous pixels that contain the recombined information. Our brains combine the information from the pixels to create an image that we recognize.

While the original digital wave could be considered non-dual, the infinite images that appear on the screen appear to be dualistic. The image of a can of cola is seen as being separate from the image of the person that is drinking it. In this manner, duality is found in non-duality as the television images are a function of the digital wave. Since the digital wave is found within the images on the screen, non-duality is found in duality.

Conclusion

If you put on a pair of red tinted sunglasses, everything that you see will appear red. If you put on a pair of green tinted sunglasses, everything that you see will appear green. The perspective that you experience wearing sunglasses is of little consequence to you because you know that your perspective is being distorted by the colored lenses. But what if you were born with your tinted sunglasses on? Given that you would not have had the opportunity to experience the world with them off, you would believe that your perspective of the world was accurate.

Every person is looking to understand something. Some people are looking to understand how they can improve themselves through self-help programs. Some people are looking to understand how they can improve their finances. There are scientist that are looking to understand the nature of black holes and outer space, and there are researchers that are looking to understand how certain biological organisms are able to fight of cancer.

Regardless of what we are seeking to understand, history has shown that we have neglected to try to understand the nature of who we are. How can we understand anything if we do not first understand ourselves. As long as we do not understand the nature of who we are, our efforts to understand the subject of our interest will be like the infant born with tinted sunglasses on.

As stated in the introduction, the purpose of this book is provide the reader with a different perspective, a perspective that is drastically different from our conventional thinking. This perspective is drastically different because it goes against everything that we were taught to believe.

A paradigm shift is a fundamental change in how we view the world. This change can occur at an individual or societal level. Examples of famous paradigm shifts in history include the view that the Earth is round, not flat, that the Earth revolves around the sun, that space-time is not fixed or objective, or the discovery of quantum mechanics. Each of these paradigm shifts were treated as "fringe" ideas that met much resistance. The gradual acceptance of these paradigm shifts eventually led to their widespread acceptance. As life changing as paradigm shifts have been on our lives, no paradigm shift has ever challenged the nature of who we are as human beings. As long as we view ourselves as being separate from the rest of life, we will engage in a mindset that is dominated by the beliefs that exploiting our planet and other people is justified in the name of progress, religion, or political expediency.

Every challenge that we face, both individually and collectively, is due to our inability to identify with others and our own fears of scarcity. The only reason why exploitation of others and the planet exists is because of our lack of compassion and our need to put our self-interest first. We lack compassion for others because we are unable to connect with ourselves. We place our self-interest first because we feel insignificant unless we can express overt power. That we, as a species, have difficulty identifying with others, or overcoming our self-interest, is not an accident. As we discussed in this book, we are all tapping into the collective consciousness. Nothing in life is eternal, except for life itself. Every time we take on a new perspective, we are contributing to the changing of the collective consciousness.

Consciousness is dynamic and ever changing. What fuels that change is the input that we give it through our thoughts. The evolution of consciousness starts with the evolution of thought within the individual.

Being able to experience yourself as multidimensional beings changes both you and the rest of humanity. With thoughtful self-inquiry, how can we dispute that we are part of a greater awareness while simultaneously being a physical being. If you apply what you have learned from this book with an open mind, and a persistent but patient attitude, you will be on the vanguard of a consciousness revolution.

The End

Dear reader,

I sincerely hope that you feel inspired by the 21 METAPHYSICAL SECRETS and enjoyed the 9 Do-It-Yourself Energy Experiments.

Before you close this book I´d like to ask you for a favor to leave an honest review on amazon. It´d be greatly appreciated.

Just click here to leave a review on amazon.

Thank you and good luck!

Erik Tao

21 SECRETS OF ATTRACTING MONEY

Metaphysical Insights For Physical And Spiritual Wealth—Including 9 Do-It-Yourself Energy Experiments

Table Of Contents:

Introduction

"You are the creator; you create with your every thought." This is the key to the law of attraction. Whatever you wish to manifest in your life starts with your thoughts."

—Abraham Hicks

Imagine for a while how wonderful it would be to live a life filled with your deepest desires and dreams—after all, you have all the wealth in the world to enjoy your time to the fullest. Imagine living a fulfilling, stress-free, and gratifying life without any financial constraints. Imagine being the best at what you do and unlocking your true destiny to build wealth, prosperity, and abundance. Perhaps you're now asking yourself, *Can I really live this life?*

Fortunately, the key to unlocking your destiny is in your hands. You hold the steering wheel of your life and can maneuver it in any direction of your choosing. You build your destiny through your thoughts, words, and actions. The wealth creation metaphysical concepts I explain in this book are unfailing, proven, and absolute if done with the correct intention and a powerful belief.

I've had several people come up to me and ask, "Does this really work?" I ask them in turn, "Do you have it in you to make it work?" Nothing works on its own. You have to *make* it work. These are proven principles of wealth creation and abundance successfully used by countless people across the world to build physical as well as spiritual wealth, and there's your proof: it works! However, whether it works for you or not depends on how much you are willing to make it work! Everything works if *you* work. You are completely in control of your destiny and have the potential to attract all you desire in life if you truly believe you are worthy of receiving it.

I don't know where you are currently in life. Maybe it was your last few dollars that you spent buying this book, or you may already be on your way to building riches and fortunes. Irrespective of what you have or don't have currently, you possess the power to control your life and create your destiny. The law of attraction and other powerful metaphysical money attraction secrets have no exceptions. The exception and limitations are in your beliefs and intentions. If your belief is unfailing, these laws will never let you down. When you are in alignment with your deepest desires, it is easy to attract them. Remember, the universe responds to your thought frequencies and energies. Wealth and abundance don't come from outside you. It resides in you in the form of thoughts, energies, and actions.

Before you hold something you desire in your hand, you strongly create energy to attract it within you. You believe and operate with the mindset that it is yours. To bring it into your life, you believe you truly deserve it. This is what the law of attraction and other metaphysical principles are all about. It is about energy transmitted through a strong intention, which helps you attract and manifest your desires.

What can I get from this book? I don't promise overnight riches. No one can. Whoever does is making a big fool out of you. You won't go from ten dollars to a million dollars overnight. However, by applying these wealth creation secrets consistently with the right intention over a period of time, you can engender a transformation in the relationship between you and wealth. You will open your mind and heart to attract abundance, you will align your energies with the universe to receive even more prosperity, and you will increase your chances of living the life of your dreams. Not a bad deal!

We all seek to attract the good things in life, yet we are always playing slaves and victims of destiny. Funnily enough, people will wish for all the wonderful things to happen without even realizing that the power to create what they wish for is within them.

You will understand the principles of metaphysics that elucidate how frequencies created in your mind through thoughts can be utilized to manifest wealth and abundance. If you fixate on a single thing, emotion, desire, or feeling over an extended period, it transforms into your reality. These concepts work equally for everyone if you have the power to believe in them!

Think about it. Why is it that some people have everything in life? They have the best of jobs or businesses, money comes to them effortlessly through multiple channels, they enjoy the best interpersonal relationships—all that while others struggle to go through life, barely making ends meet. If these principles are similar for everyone, why doesn't everyone receive what he or she desires?

Creating wealth and abundance using metaphysical techniques is a powerful process that originates in your mind. The unfortunate aspect of this is that a majority of people are not even aware that they themselves are responsible for the lack of resources in their life. They do not know that they are attracting their own misery owing to their thoughts. We often blame our destiny, other people, or circumstances, among other things, for our misfortunes, little realizing that these have been created by us through both our conscious and subconscious thoughts.

It is a challenge to take the self-limiting beliefs you've held since childhood by their horns and tackle them. If you've been led to believe as children that money is a bad thing, or that it makes people bad, or that you don't need it since there are other more important things in life, you'll have to bring about a huge shift in the way you view money. These self-limiting and incorrect beliefs are so deeply ingrained in us at times that it goes unquestioned and we accept it as truth. When you accept these beliefs as the truth, you don't enjoy a healthy relationship with money, which is why it eludes you throughout your life. I know many who were raised in less than privileged homes and grew up with the belief that "money makes people bad" or "it is the root cause of all evils." These people never really attract wealth and abundance until they consciously align their spiritual energy to attract and wholeheartedly welcome money.

Before you begin reading any further, analyze your beliefs and relationship with wealth. If it's anything other than healthy and positive, you won't be able to make any of these principles work for you. It is your beliefs, energies, intentions, and actions alone that are responsible for attracting or repelling wealth and abundance. In effect, you are pushing away money that is coming your way simply due to the beliefs you hold about it. Isn't this grossly unfortunate?

Stop whatever you are doing right now and make a note about your beliefs regarding money and wealth. Go back to the source. Where did your views and beliefs about wealth originate? Why is money energy negative for you? What are the positive changes you can make in your life, your loved ones' lives, and the world at large with money energy? Do you hold these feelings or emotions about wealth yourself or have they been influenced by another person? Work on transforming your beliefs, feelings, and thoughts about money and you may notice a miraculous transformation in the way it flows to you. Remember, you alone are the author and creator of your destiny!

Secret No. 1:
Believe

"The feelings of our desires much precede its manifestation."

—Sarah Prout

Do you realize that there are probably thousands of thoughts going on in your mind in a single day? These thoughts have the power to impact your reality and destiny. If you aren't happy with where you are currently in life, you can change your destiny by reshaping your thoughts to manifest your deepest desires. One of the biggest reason people do not attract wealth is that they believe they don't deserve it or that it is something that is beyond their destiny. They believe they aren't as fortunate as the wealthy and successful. In short, their energies are not aligned to attract abundance. It starts with developing a wealthy mindset, and a mindset that has incorrect or self-limiting ideas about money isn't geared for attracting wealth.

We discussed in the Introduction how some people grow up with limiting beliefs about wealth and money. If you believe money makes people bad or that it is the cause of all evil, you share an unhealthy relationship with money. You are therefore, in effect, not aligning yourself to receive wealth from the universe.

The number one secret to manifesting anything in your life, not just money, is to operate with the belief that it is already yours. You don't see it as a far-fetched desire or wish that will be fulfilled in the future. You think, act, feel, and behave like you already have it.

Our thoughts, emotions, and feelings carry a very powerful energy frequency. When you believe something is already yours, you are releasing a strong energy frequency into the universe. Now, on a metaphysical level, the universe is nothing but a mass of energy surrounding us. When you send powerful signals into the universe, it responds with a matching frequency, which means you attract even more of what you strongly believe is already yours.

The feelings or emotions you experience about your deepest desires is the most powerful force in the process of manifestation. These feelings interact with the universe at an energy level. If you feel like something you desire is already yours, your thoughts, feelings, actions, and behavior are in alignment with a positive energy. This positive energy frequency communicates with the outer universe, which then matches your energy frequency by sending you precisely what you desire. Anything your mind conceives, the universe has the power to manifest!

While thinking, feeling, and acting like something is already yours will attract matching energy frequencies from the universe, when you operate with an "I want *something*" belief, you are merely reinforcing the lack of it in your life. You want money because you don't have enough money in your life. This sends a "lack of" energy frequency into the universe, and you end up receiving even more of its lack.

However, in contrast, when you believe that richness, wealth, and abundance are already yours, you send an energy frequency of wealth, abundance, and prosperity and end up attracting even more of it. Do you get the picture? If you think you are poor, you will attract even more poverty. If you believe you have to work really hard to make ends meet, you'll attract even more of this situation. When we perpetually obsess about the lack of something or desperately wanting something (thus reinforcing the lack of it in our life), we continue to lack it.

When do you say you want something? When you don't have something! If you say you want money, you are in effect telling the universe that you don't have enough of it. Start thinking you have everything you want before you truly bring it in your life! This is the biggest secret of the law of attraction.

If you want to attract more wealth and abundance, start by believing it is already yours. Act like you are a millionaire. Dress like one! Talk like one! Observe how millionaires talk, feel, respond to others, and conduct themselves. In your head, you must already be a millionaire because only then will you end up being one.

Secret No. 2:
Subconsciousness

Images have a huge power when it comes to conveying our desires to the universe with intention and purposefulness. They are probably ten times more powerful than words. When you visualize your desires, you don't just send strong energy frequency signals to the universe, you also send them to your subconscious mind, which is a highly potent tool when it comes to manifesting your desires.

When a thought, idea, image, or feeling is strongly imprinted in the human subconscious mind, it guides our actions in alignment with this thought, which helps us create exactly what we desire. How do you send the right signals to the universe and your subconscious mind? Through the power of images and visuals!

Visualization exercises and guided visualization is best practiced early in the morning or just before going to bed. These are the hours when your subconscious mind is most active and can be activated to unlock your true destiny. If you practice visualization exercises just before going to bed, you will give your subconscious mind the right ideas to play around with since it is most active when our conscious mind is asleep.

To practice self-visualization exercises or guided visualization meditation, sit in a distraction-free, quiet, and comfortable place. You can infuse positive energy into the space by lighting candles or burning incense. Assume a relaxed posture. Allow the stress in your body and mind to melt away before you begin. Get into a more positive frame of mind. Close your eyes, and now, start imaging through your mind's eye.

Start by visualizing what you want in explicit detail. Remember, the key is being detailed. The more detailed and precise your visualizations, the greater are your chances of manifesting exactly what you desire.

Let's say for instance you want to increase your company's profits. Be exact when you prescribe visualizations. How much do you want to increase your annual or monthly profits by? Even an increase of $0.50 is an increase. So, if you don't visualize how much you want the profits to increase, you aren't giving the universe or your subconscious mind the exact ideas to work with.

Visualize you profit statement with a profit of a million dollars if that is what you want. How does the profit statement look? How are you holding it in your hand? How do you feel when your company makes a profit of a million? Experiencing these feelings and emotions is integral to the process of manifesting your desires.

Make your visualizations a multi-sensory experience if you want to boost your chances of manifesting what you want. How does your office look after you make a million dollars? How are you and your employees dressed? How does your workplace smell, look, sound, and feel?

There are plenty of guided visualization meditation exercises for attracting more money. The mental images you create through the process of visualization are a projection of your future, which you go through as if it is your present. We learned the importance of believing that something is already ours before we can manifest it. Now, create mental images or visuals of your money goals being fulfilled. Keep in mind, this is the movie of your life. You can't be passive spectators. You play the central role and visualize yourself doing exactly what you want to manifest in life. See yourself enjoying the results of what you desired.

If you want to be wealthy and prosperous enough to travel around the world, see yourself at exotic locations across the planet. Visualize yourself traveling to your dream destinations. If you want money to buy your dream home, imagine your home in explicit detail. How about sitting comfortably by the fireplace and relishing a cup of coffee in your dream home? Or holding the steering wheel of the luxury car you plan to buy? Or sitting in a tropical paradise with a drink in your hand? Give your mind and the universe powerful images to play with so their task in helping you manifest these desires becomes easier. Feel, think, and mentally experience everything you desire.

Visualize the amount of money you wish to make. Do not visualize it as if it's something that you are receiving in the future. See it right now, in your bank account. The exact digits you want. Complete the experience and absorb the feeling of how this figure feels on your bank statement. How exactly do you feel when you have this figure in your bank account?

I know it isn't easy to visualize you are a millionaire when you are currently struggling to pay for your next meal. However, this is exactly what separates the wealthy from the strugglers.

The wealthy don't let their current circumstances and challenges spill over into their beliefs about the future. They operate with a powerful belief and intention that it's only a matter of time before they manifest the wealth and life of their destiny. See the magic digit in your account like it exists currently even if you have nothing. This is precisely why some people make the law of attraction work wonderfully for them while others struggle with doing the same.

Experience the exact emotions and feelings that a person does when he has a million dollars on his or her bank account. In fact, go a few steps ahead and start thinking about how you can use the money. What are the things you plan to buy with it? How will you invest it to create even more wealth? Don't most millionaires do this? You are one right now and, like a true-blue millionaire, you should think about how you plan to utilize your financial resources.

I'll share a small story here. A young boy grew up in such poverty that at one point in his life, his family couldn't even afford to live in a proper home. They occupied a trailer parked on the lawns of a relative' house. He toiled for eight hours daily at a factory to fund his education and help support his family.

When things became tough, he dropped out from high school and started taking up odd jobs to feed his family. He began doing stand-up comedy gigs at the local club only to be heckled by the audience.

Fed up of his wretched and miserable life, the lad moved to Hollywood at the age of 21, and the first step he took when he reached Hollywood probably impacted his entire life. The young man drove right up Hollywood hills in his worn-out Toyota and parked it where he could take sweeping views of the entertainment industry hub along with its dazzling lights. In his head, he visualized himself to be a part of this dream world, entertaining people and making them laugh.

Instead of simply imagining it, the young man did something unthinkable. As a physical reminder of his dream and the exact moment he experienced this desire, he wrote a check to himself for 10 million dollars. His current bank balance was a different story altogether, but that didn't stop him from visualizing his future as if he had already received this amount of money. The check was for "acting services rendered." The young man kept this check as a physical reminder of his dreams in his wallet. Each time he went for a work-related meeting or audition, the check went with him.

The actor went on to receive a princely advance-signing amount for an upcoming film and subsequently went on to make not just his 10 million dollars but much more in the years succeeding. He was confident in his belief that there was no other way but to become a millionaire. He didn't award himself the option of failure. He was dead sure he'd be a millionaire one day. This young man was none other than Jim Carrey. This is a real-life example of the power of visualization and using the power of your intentions to create your destiny.

You have to think something is already yours and visualize it like it is yours before you can transform it into reality.

Secret No. 3:
Gratefulness

A grateful heart is the most powerful magnet for attracting blessings. There is plenty of power in gratefulness. When you are thankful for something, at a metaphysical level, you are sending a strong positive frequency into the universe. It demonstrates the universe that you have positive frequencies about possessing something in abundance, which helps you attract even more of it. If you want to create more wealth and abundance, be grateful for the money you have, however little it seems at the moment.

If you don't perceive what you presently own with gratitude, there will only be a slim chance of multiplying it. Blessings and complaints both multiply. If you gripe about the lack of something or display an element of ingratitude for what you already have, you are not aligning the energy frequency to receive more of it from the universe. Be thankful for the money and possessions you already own to draw more of them into your realm of reality.

Make a gratitude journal today. At the end of each day, write about 10 things that happened during the day or 10 gifts you feel thankful or blessed to enjoy in your life. Ensure that you add 10 new things to be grateful for each day. It can be anything from the eyes with which you see the beautiful world around you to the feet with which you walk to your workplace. It can be your hands, the roof above your head, the loaf of bread you baked, and your car—just about everything you can and should feel grateful for. Express thankfulness for everything that money can buy you to multiply your wealth and assets.

If your mind is constantly operating with a feeling of being thankful for the wealth you have, your feelings, thoughts, and emotions will be aligned with a powerful energy of thankfulness, thus giving you even more things to be grateful for. Gratitude signifies abundance. By being thankful, you are reinforcing your abundance and attracting even more abundance your way.

Another super wealth attraction tip is to keep a gratitude rock in your pocket, wallet, or purse all the time. Keep it somewhere you can physically and frequently come into contact with it. You can also place it on your work desk or wherever you can spot it prominently throughout the day. Each time you touch the gratitude rock, find something you've bought with your money that you are grateful for. It can be your house, a piece of clothing, a car, a book—anything that you are thankful for receiving from the universe through the means of money. Do this a few times throughout the day, especially before going to bed and on awakening. Think about the wealth and possessions you are truly thankful for.

To create more of what you want, you have to display thankfulness for what you already own.

Don't reserve your thankfulness for the future or when you get what you desire. Be thankful for what you have now.

If you have unpaid bills, avoid cribbing about them. It only releases more negativity and attracts even more unpaid bills. Instead, write on the bills prominently, "Thank you universe (or any energy or spiritual force you believe in) for helping me pay this bill." Feel a genuine sense of thankfulness and gratitude for the services you enjoy. Being thankful for the services and feeling happy about paying for them are the keys to clear your bills. If you keep viewing them as a burden or from a point of thanklessness, you'll seldom be able to pay them off. Gratitude is the magic word! Change your relationship with your bills, view these services as a blessing, and you'll seldom be short on money to clear them.

A gratitude rock helps you focus your energies on the present and helps you draw attention to the current moment and blessings. It helps you experience thankfulness for the now and what you have on you presently (clothes, pen, book) to multiply your blessings.

It also helps to switch your thoughts from neutral or negative to positive. If you are in an unpleasant mood, simply being thankful for what you have can instantly lift your spirits or elevate your mood.

You can pick up stone or rock that resonates with you from around a stream, park, or road. I'd strongly recommend selecting a stone that you instantly connect with on a deeper level. You can also buy crystals such as citrine that are known to attract abundance.

Secret No. 4:
Affirmations

Affirmations are positive statements that are said or written multiple times to influence our subconscious mind into believing something as the truth. Words that are spoken in repetition have the potential to firmly embed mental images on the human subconscious mind, thus guiding or influencing our actions in the correct and positive direction. These words motivate, drive, and energize you into creating what you desire.

The mental visuals created by saying these affirmations repeatedly are capable of bringing about a rapid shift in thoughts, ideas, feelings, and actions, thus channelizing our mental energies towards manifesting what we desire. You truly imbibe the feelings and emotions of what you keep saying, which is why these affirmations work wonderfully for manifesting money, wealth, and abundance.

The human subconscious mind is incapable of differentiating between reality and imagination. It believes whatever is imprinted into it as reality. Subsequently, it guides your actions in line with this belief. When you keep saying you are rich, prosperous, and wealthy in a loop, irrespective of what your current financial position is, your subconscious mind accepts it as the truth.

It then guides your actions in line with being wealthy, prosperous, and abundant. You are activating your subconscious mind to operate from a point of scarcity to abundance with a few words or phrases.

Always say your affirmations in the present tense to ascertain that it unlocks the power of your subconscious mind and gets it to guide your actions in the direction of wealth and abundance.

Don't say something as if you are going to accomplish it in the future, such as "I will be rich and prosperous" or "I am going to be wealthy soon." This only reinforces the present lack of it in your life. Your goals aren't placed beyond your reach in the future, they are already yours now!

Stick to positive words and phrases while creating your affirmations. It shouldn't contain any negative words. Our subconscious mind and the universal one cannot at the metaphysical energy level relate to the concept of "not." It simply throws away the no or not and focuses on the energy attached to the words and phrases used.

For example, if you say "I don't want to be poor," the subconscious mind and universal energy will discard the "don't" and focus on the energy attached to poor, thus bringing even more poverty your way. Instead, say "I am rich, wealthy, and abundant." Use only positive words and phrases about money.

Keep your affirmations personal. Use affirmations that feel good and right to you instead of simply borrowing them from someone else, though you can look on the internet for inspiration. However, you must be able to connect with them on a personal level. Create affirmations that feel right for you.

These positive statements should also be specific, detailed, and unambiguous. Avoid affirming more than one desire in a single statement. You can use different affirmations for different desires. However, clubbing them together in a single sentence can send your subconscious mind and the universe on a wild goose chase. The more detailed and precise your affirmations, the greater are your chances of manifesting it. Reinforce the benefits of manifesting your desires. Precise images help in clarifying your desires to the subconscious mind. Vague affirmations create vague results.

For instance, if you want to increase your business profits this year, you can't simply say "business profits increase." Even an increase in $1 is an increase! How much do you want to increase the profit by? $500? $1000? $100,000? Say "my business profits have increased by (the exact amount)." The ideal time to say your affirmations is when you can see yourself saying it. This multiplies their manifesting energy. Say them while applying make-up, shaving, or getting ready to go to work in the morning. See yourself saying these powerful affirmations while also experiencing the feelings as you do.

Affirmations can also be written several times in an affirmation journal. Allow the feeling to sink while you write. Preferably, use a notebook and a pen instead of a technological application. The process of physically writing something has more impact on the mind because your nerves are directly connected to the subconscious.

Ensure you say your affirmations as many times as possible throughout the day—the more, the better because it will only end up reinforcing the idea more powerfully within your subconscious mind. Say them for a minimum of 20 times, thrice a day. Keep saying it until your subconscious mind accepts it as your true destiny. Make affirmation usage the practice or habit of a lifetime.

Following are a few wealth and abundance affirmations that you can start using right away to attract wealth, money, and abundance.

1. Money, prosperity, and abundance are pouring into my life.
2. I openly embrace and accept wealth, money, and prosperity right now.
3. I am truly grateful to the universe for the overflowing wealth, riches, and abundance in my life.
4. Money flows to me easily and effortlessly.
5. I am a money, wealth, and abundance magnet.
6. Whatever I put my hand on is converted into wealth, riches, and prosperity.

7. I am thankful for limitless riches and wealth that flows my way.

These are just a few examples. Create your own affirmations based exactly on what you want and say them in the present tense by using positive words and phrases.

Secret No. 5:
Vision Board
(Energy Experiment)

One of the most powerful metaphysical techniques for manifesting your dream destiny is the creation of a vision board. A vision board is a physical or virtual board that represents all our goals, desires, wishes, and visions pictorially. Through images, our vision board depicts what we want in life. We've seen in an earlier chapter how visuals containing powerful energy transmit the right energy frequencies to the universe and our subconscious mind.

By representing your dreams and desires through visuals, you are strengthening and stimulating your innermost emotions because the human mind responds powerfully to visual stimulation. Your feelings and emotions related to the desire then become the vibrational energy that triggers the law of attraction!

Following are some tips to make the most of your vision board.

1. Place your vision board in a place where you can prominently spot it multiple times during the day. It is best if that's the first thing you can see on awakening each morning. Visualization is known to tap into the creative potential of your subconscious mind while programming the brain to spot resources that can lead you closer to the goals you probably didn't notice earlier. Through the metaphysical principles of the law of attraction, your vision board magnetizes or attracts you to situations, people, and opportunities that are needed to manifest your goal. Thus, if your vision board is filled with visuals of being rich, prosperous, and wealthy, you'll increase your chances of magnetizing people and

resources that lead you towards accomplishing your financial goals.

2. Be judicious about the images you pick. Look everywhere from the internet to magazines to brochures and calendars to personal photo albums. Make a beautiful collage out of all the images. Use images that you can connect with on a deeper level. Make the vision board more personalized by adding comic strips, movie dialogues, song lyrics, book quotes, and motivational quotes by famous people that inspire you. I know people who like to use stickers and make sketches to make their vision board even more personalized and power-packed. Do whatever inspires you each time you look at it because you are activating the power of your subconscious mind to send powerful signals to the universe for manifesting your desires.

3. I would also suggest including positive affirmations about how you feel. Remember

your vision board isn't merely about things but the feelings these things evoke in you. Add plenty of positive feelings to the vision board such as abundant, joyful, wealthy, prosperous, financially free, rich, and so on. You should experience these feelings each time you glance towards the vision board. Several successful people I know are in the habit of scanning their vision board just before practicing their visualization exercises and retiring for the day. This helps prompt your subconscious mind to create new insights and ideas while your conscious mind is asleep at night. You'll wake up with a burst of energy and enthusiasm to succeed. Also, you will be guided by your subconscious mind to identify and act on opportunities that lead you closer to your wealth goals.

4. While there's no limit to what you seek from the universe (and what it bestows you in turn), avoid cluttering your vision board

with too many goals and wishes. Keep it limited to 5-6 goals at a time.

5. Get creative with your vision board. I know several people who add several materials, elements, and mediums to their vision board to make it even more power-packed. They use everything from ticket stubs, flowers, brochures, menus, feathers, cloth pieces, and plenty of stuff to represent their true desires.

Secret No. 6:
Switch Words
(Energy Experiment)

Switchwords are similar to mantras that are chanted to bring about a switch in the energy of your subconscious mind. Though psychotherapist Sigmund Freud first noted the concept of words impacting our subconscious mind, James Mangam created the concept of Switchwords in his book, *The Secret of Perfect Living*. Though the public wasn't ready for this concept at that time, it came back with a bang recently.

Switchwords are nothing but regular, everyday words that are linked to the vibrational frequency that these words generate. They work on the same principles as affirmations. When you keep saying these words in a loop, they talk directly to our subconscious mind. Thus, the power words help in clearing negative blocks that impede our success and activate our capacity to manifest wealth, abundance, creativity, success, and anything else we desire. If there is a negative thought debris that tells you that you don't deserve to be rich and prosperous held within your subconscious mind, Switchwords will help clear it and bring about a more positive transformation in your thought frequencies, thus impacting your actions and opportunities. At times, there are numbers attached to these words, and they come with their own frequency and add to the power of Switchboards.

Switchwords can be used in several ways:

- You can say them repeatedly throughout the day. Say it 20-30 times at least thrice a day to make the most of its powers.
- Switchwords can also be written several times throughout the day.
- They can be used in your artwork or writing.

- Meditate with Switchwords that resonate with you or that you can connect with on a deeper level.
- Some spiritual experts also suggest charging and drinking water (or labeling the water you drink) with these Switchwords.
- They can be written on pieces of paper and kept under your pillow while sleeping.
- Switchwords can also be written on the left side of your body.

The most important thing about using these magic words is they have to be used with the right belief and intention to work. Here are some Switchwords that can help you attract money, wealth, prosperity, riches, and abundance.

- *Find-Count-Divine*: For miracles related to money
- *Shreem*: For attracting wealth and riches
- *Count-Count-Count-520*: For enjoying financial freedom

- *Together-Find-Count-Divine*: For miraculous money-making
- *Add-Count*: To increase or multiply money

Secret No. 7:
Red Wallet

"Abundance isn't something we acquire. It is something we tune into."

–Wayne Dyer

Though it sounds strange at the onset, the color of your wallet or the energy emitted through it can also impact your chances of having money and riches. The Ancient Chinese science of Feng Shui, which talks about the placement and nature of objects in attracting the most positive and powerful energies, lists a few colors that can help your money-manifestation process.

Wallets and purses are known to hold energy because this is where the money you carry is primarily placed. There are plenty of Feng Shui tips to attract money and abundance, starting with the color of your wallet or purse.

According to Feng Shui, since your wallet holds money energy, it should always be treated well. Keep it in great condition, discard all unwanted clutter from it, and keep it in a safe space back home to attract more positive *qi* energy.

Colors possess energy too like everything else, and they stimulate certain psychological responses within our mind. Color psychology is real because it impacts our thoughts, feelings, and emotions at a subconscious level. For instance, notice how the color blue calms you down or green refreshes and rejuvenates your senses. Why not leverage the power of colors when it comes to attracting wealth and abundance?

Red is considered to be the most auspicious color in Feng Shui for attracting money and abundance. It represents the fire element. If you think red is too bright a color for a purse or wallet, try using a combination of reddish black. Red gives you the energy, dynamism, and passion for attracting more wealth-creation opportunities.

The color red also symbolizes strength, power, and success, which means you'll be less likely to spend frivolously. Red can drive or channel your own energy, enthusiasm, and spirit. In Feng Shui, red wallets aren't just known to enhance wealth prospects but also offer good fortune and protection.

Other than red, gold is also considered a classic color for magnetizing wealth, abundance, and riches. The color gold traditionally corresponds with abundance, luck, good fortune, and positivity. The energy, vibrations, and spirit of the carrier that holds your money can considerably impact your wealth-attraction process.

Whether it is energy related to the color red or gold or simply your intention that expects to wholeheartedly receive more money and riches when you use these colors, it is known to work!

Here are some tips to make your wallet luck work for you:

- Keep your purse or wallet clean, neat, and organized all the time. Avoid retaining receipts, expired cards, and other unwanted objects as these impact your wallet energy negatively.

- Store your bills in a well-organized manner to ensure they are placed in the same direction in numerical order.

- Avoid placing your purse or wallet on the floor or ground. Always keep it in a well-organized and positively energized space. Toilets are a big no-no.

- Immediately replace your old and worn-out wallet. You are not holding the right money energy by using a wallet that has undergone wear and tear. Renew your money luck with a new purse or wallet.

- Ensure that your wallet is never empty. Always have some money in your wallet or purse if you want to attract even more money. At the same time, never overstuff your purse or wallet. Leave some space for more money. Also, ascertain that your wallet is long enough to prevent bills from folding and avoid picking wallets that are strangely shaped. Just ensure it is a regular, long wallet to enable you to keep bills straight.

- Don't let other people borrow your wallet or purse, and never use secondhand purses or wallets. Your money energy should be kept pure and personal.

Secret No. 8:
Generosity

This isn't just another do-gooder act for earning brownie points. It is a very powerful principle connected to the law of attraction that can help you attract even more when you give.

When you demonstrate generosity and help others, you are only reinforcing your abundance. When do you give or help others with money and other things? When we have excess resources! Some of the world's wealthiest leaders, entrepreneurs, and celebrities helm charitable causes or practice philanthropy because they have plenty of wealth to distribute among the less privileged. This, in turn, helps them attract even more wealth, abundance, and good fortune.

At a metaphysical level, you are communicating an energy of abundance to the universe when you engage in charity or generosity. You operate from a point of abundance and not a point of scarcity, which brings about a huge transformation in your energy. Your acts of kindness and generosity set the stage for you to receive even more from the infinite universal sources.

When we practice acts of generosity, our energy shifts from a state of lack to one of abundance, and a simple shift in energy helps activate our receiving energy.

The simplest and best way to begin is by helping those less fortunate than you. It can be help in the form of money, things, or even service. The help or act of charity can be extended towards a single person or a sector of society. The universe, on a metaphysical energy level, is not concerned about how much you give. Irrespective of how big or little you contribute, you increase your money and good fortune attraction energy.

Don't give with the selfish intention of getting it back from the universe. That is counterproductive to the process of money and wealth manifestation. Set the right intention while giving. When you help someone from a point of genuine compassion, goodness, and love, you create a larger space for receiving abundance, wealth, and happiness. Aim to give selflessly and out of genuine kindness without expecting anything in return, and you'll watch your wealth multiply.

Secret No. 9:
Feng Shui

Like we discussed in an earlier chapter, Feng Shui is an Ancient Chinese discipline that dates back more than 3000 years. It was created to balance *qi* (energies) within a specific space. This energy is said to be directly responsible for attracting health, wealth, harmony, and good fortune in our life.

The principles of Feng Shui are rooted in the Taoist view of nature. The principles mentioned in this chapter can be widely used for stimulating the circulation of money, prosperity, and abundance in your life. Here are six simple yet effective ways to align yourself optimally with wealth attraction positions.

1. Keep the kitchen clean. Kitchens are directly linked to your capacity to attract money in Feng Shui. Everything from the refrigerator

to the pantry to the stove should be kept immaculate by storing only the food that is used. Use every burner on the stove. Also, get rid of clutter from the countertops, tables, and islands in the kitchen. A clutter-free, well-organized, and clean kitchen becomes a magnet for wealth.

2. Discard all clutter. This one's huge in Feng Shui because the discipline is based primarily on energies within a space. Space represents opportunities, which means a cluttered space invariably signifies blocked opportunities. By getting rid of unwanted clutter, you'll free the way for money, abundance, and opportunities at the vibration level.

3. Use mirrors and water features. The condition of water in your home directly impacts your finances according to Feng Shui. Never have leaking taps, dripping pipes, or stagnant water in and around the house as it represents wealth leaving your

abode. Broken fountains and other water bodies are not conducive to wealth creation. Avoid water-based art and mirrors that are placed on a height. There should be no hanging mirrors and water-based art above your bed too. It doesn't align with attracting wealth and prosperity.

4. Pay attention to your home office table. Never place it directly against a wall as this represents blocked creative flow, opportunities, and potential. The larger the space opposite your desk, the more opportunities you will attract according to Feng Shui. Arrange your chair so you face an expansive view or keep visitor chairs in front of your desk for attracting money, opportunities, and abundance.

5. Beautify your front door. Wealth and prosperity energies are said to be at your front door. Always keep your porch area and front door squeaky clean. Avoid keeping broken bulbs or dying plants at the entrance

as these signify dead or blocked energy that acts as an obstacle to the flow of money. Increase your money energy by sprucing up the front door, porch, and walkway. Add pretty flowering pots and a dazzling porch light. The area should be well-lit for welcoming greater wealth and prosperity into the household. In Ancient Chinese Feng Shui philosophy, the front door is referred to as the "mouth of *qi*." Its quality and auspicious energy are integral to the Feng Shui of the entire house. You can also use auspicious Feng Shui symbols at the entrance for attracting wealth, good fortune, and abundance.

6. Use the power of your Feng Shui wealth area. According to the traditional school of Feng Shui, your home or office's southeast corner is your wealth or money corner. The element that rules money and wealth in Feng Shui is wood. Using a flowing water feature like a fountain in your wealth area can activate or

facilitate the energy for flowing money and abundance. Placing a jade plant in the area is also a good idea. Use small icons or symbols representing money to increase prosperity. Many people like placing a wealth box in their money or wealth area to activate their money-making power. Use simple materials such as crystals, coins, gems, or anything that signifies money and prosperity. Place all the items in a finely decorated money box, which can in turn be kept in your wealth area.

Secret No. 10:
Hollywood

Earlier, we talked about the famous Jim Carrey incident. When Carrey was a young, struggling comedian trying to make ends meet by performing small gigs in Hollywood, he almost gave up on his dreams of becoming a professional actor. After being heckled off the stage following an act at an open microphone session in Los Angeles, he was completely disillusioned and thought he could never be a professional comedian—ever.

Jim sat alone on top of the Mulholland Drive reflecting upon his failures. Suddenly, he did the unthinkable. Jim pulled out a check from his checkbook and wrote himself a check of $10 million. Yes, his current fortune was nowhere close to that figure. The check was written for "acting services rendered."

As I described before, this famous check went everywhere with him. In 1995, after the runaway success of his movies *Dum and Dumber* and *The Mask*, his net worth has gone up to $20 million. That is the power of writing yourself a check. You are carrying positive and powerful energies in your purse or wallet when you write yourself one.

The energies transmitted through this check of abundance have the power to drive your actions and help you seize opportunities at an intuitive, subconscious level. Write yourself a check today of a precise amount and place it in your wallet, purse, or handbag all the time. You'll end up attracting plenty of money-making opportunities!

Secret No. 11:
Emotions

My friend who wasn't so wealthy once upon a time had a habit that we all found strange back when we didn't know the powerful principles of the law of attraction and money manifestation. Every once in a while, she'd purchase stuff that would make her feel rich, wealthy, and prosperous. It wasn't just another self-indulgent or preposterous act. It was a way of attracting money on a deeper level. Soon enough, all the things that we thought were beyond her financial reach were easily and effortlessly affordable to her. It was the law of attraction—unfailing and absolute. She attracted all the money, wealth, and abundance in her life because she aligned her energies with being wealthy, which brought even more wealth and good fortune her way.

Every once in a while, save and buy stuff that makes you experience a compelling feeling of being rich and abundant. Splurge on that expensive perfume, designer bag, or bottle of champagne. Next, it could be a lottery ticket or an exquisite jewelry piece—just about anything that makes you feel rich.

Act like you have plenty of money. Imbibe the classy actions and mannerisms of millionaires. Once I learned these powerful money attraction tips, I used to put on my best attire even while heading to the supermarket. People look at you like you are someone rich and prosperous, and this makes you feel rich at an energetic or subconscious level. When you feel rich at a subconscious level through power dressing or accessorizing, you raise your money-attracting vibrations. It is a signal to the universe that you are ready to receive wealth and success—and are dressed up to reach places!

Another super creative tip to feel rich and prosperous is to go to a high-end shopping mall and purchase everything you desire mentally. Experience and absorb the feeling of being able to buy the costliest shoes or the most expensive bag. Get inside the feeling space of the wealthy to transmit the right energy into the universe. How does it feel to purchase everything you want? Mentally buy that $15,000 suit or the mall's most expensive watch. This simple mental act of buying everything you desire will quickly change your money frequencies from scarcity to abundance. Go on and feel like you can buy anything you wish.

Secret No. 12:
Positivity

I've lost count of the number of times I've heard people around me say "I can't afford this" or "It is too expensive for me" or "I don't have enough money to buy it." It isn't a mere coincidence that these people never end up buying the things they say they can't afford.

Stop yourself in the tracks each time you find yourself engaging in self-limiting language patterns. It does more damage to your subconscious mind and vibrations than you can imagine. Replace language patterns of fear, insecurity, and lack of something with more positive and wealthier terms that reframe your subconscious. You can something like "Yes, I will buy this soon" or "I am in the process of buying it" or "This is going to be mine pretty soon." It could also be "I have all the money in the universe to buy it" or other things along that line.

Watch out for the words and phrases you use very closely. Often, they are said so involuntarily that we don't realize their impact on our subconscious. Vocalizing your insecurities, disappointments, and fears only enforces the lack of money and abundance. When you say you can't afford something, you are creating a negative and defeatist vibration about the lack of something in your life. This disillusionment ends up making you feel even more frustrated and disillusioned, which blocks your opportunities and channels of attracting wealth at the subconscious level.

Reframe your powerful feelings and emotions' vibrations by replacing negative and self-limiting terms with winning and positive words and phrases.

I've closely observed the journey of a dynamic entrepreneur who didn't exactly have a very privileged upbringing. When she learned and started to apply the principles of the law of attraction, however, her life began to transform miraculously. Even when her business wasn't going great guns, she posted images of herself with her dream cars at fancy car showrooms only to receive a bunch of congratulatory remarks.

Some people thought it was highly ridiculous on her part to post images as if she'd bought the car when she clearly couldn't afford it. However, she didn't believe she couldn't afford it. In her mind, the universe had already manifested her desires, and it was only a matter of time before she held the steering in her hand. Astoundingly, she went on to buy all those luxury cars over a period of time as her business grew by leaps and bounds. If you want to truly activate the power of the universe in granting you your wish, never believe something is beyond your reach.

The universe will respond to this thought frequency by making the thing even further beyond your reach. Feel wonderful in your heart, mind, and soul by using positive language about money, abundance, and your dream material desires.

Secret No. 13:
Energy

Make yourself energetically aligned and attuned to wealth by using powerful wealth-attraction crystals. Crystals vibrate with the energy of wealth and abundance and are known to have powerful effects on your being. They are known to impact your mind, body, and spirit. Manifesting wealth through the power of crystals opens your heart and mind to recognizing more money-making opportunities with enthusiasm and confidence. You'll experience a greater sense of positivity and possibilities when it comes to magnetizing wealth.

Everything flows when there's passion and positive outlook. Crystals act as energetic supports when you undertake your wealth-creation journey. They are known to work in a unique way to bring more abundance, wealth, and prosperity your way. Combine your powerful intention with these success stones and you will have a wealth attraction technique that can seldom go wrong.

We all know wealth is energy. It often originates from passion, opportunities, beneficial outcomes, and hard work. Below are some of the best wealth, good fortune, and prosperity attracting crystals.

Aventurine

Aventurine is considered one of the luckiest wealth-manifesting crystals. It paves the way for abundance to flow since it symbolizes opportunities and opening doorways to new ventures. The stone will help you move into a more positive money mindset marked by opportunities and possibilities.

Citrine

Few crystals are better than citrine when it comes to curbing negative mental chatter about money. It is known as the ultimate abundance and wealth crystal for its powerful manifestation characteristics. If you want to bring more money, luck, and opportunities your way, citrine helps with its light. It facilitates opening your mindset to embrace opportunities and a positive mindset about money. It is known to be the preferred stone for manifesting since it helps accomplish intentions faster. Citrine is also referred to as the merchant stone for its ability to bring luck and prosperity to entrepreneurs.

Pyrite

Pyrite is perfect for those who tend to feel they aren't worthy of being rich or don't deserve abundance. This dazzling crystal resembles gold with its sparkling, mirror-like appearance. Each time you look at the stone, you'll be inspired to believe on an energetic level that you are worthy of being wealthy and prosperous.

Considered one of the most auspicious crystals for attracting money luck, pyrite is also known to help a person overcome financial hardships and magnetize wealth. It lends you more wisdom, positivity, and confidence when it comes to making important financial decisions. Thus, it guides a person's wealth accumulation in a more positive, subtle, and broader way. You'll find the perspective of your relationship with money transforming drastically.

Note that energized crystals (energized by a professional healer or spiritual master or under the guidance of one) are one of the best ways to attract wealth.

Secret No. 14:
Bills

We've discussed this briefly earlier, but a person who doesn't show their bills the required love and gratitude seldom attracts wealth. Each time a bill lands in your mailbox or email, do not view it as a burden. Like everything else, your bills possess energy. When you express disappointment or annoyance at having to clear another bill, you are increasing your chances of landing in even greater debt because the universe is responding to you with a frequency that matches your own thoughts.

Ensure that you mentally show your bills some love. Express thankfulness to the universe for the wonderful services that you received for those bills. Would you able to speak on the phone or use the internet if your service provider didn't offer you a reliable network? Would you be able to cook or enjoy the benefits of electricity if you weren't offered energy resources by your energy or power service provider? Would you able to fill gas in your car if your credit card didn't help you get by until your salary was credited? Be thankful for all the services you enjoyed in exchange for these bills.

Write "thank you for helping me pay this bill" even if you don't currently have the means to clear it. You are emitting a positive energy signal into the universe about paying the bill, thus increasing your chances of paying the bill soon. If you view it as a troublesome burden, it becomes even more of a burden.

I know people who draw little red hearts on their bills and use these as affirmations of their wealth and prosperity. This allows even more richness, wealth, and abundance to flow their way. Drawing symbols of love and gratitude on the bills and feeling a powerful emotion of thankfulness while doing it will help you pay these bills promptly.

Never send negative energy to your bills. Reframe your perspective of paying bills as an inconvenience to one of gratitude and thankfulness. View these services as a blessing to build up positive energy about them. A simple shift in your perspective can create the most unexpected miracles. Also, keep in mind that over 80% of the world's population survives on under $10 a day and doesn't have access to the services you enjoy. Give that a thought and be grateful for your bills!

Secret No. 15:
Rejoice
(Energy Experiment)

Yes, finders are indeed keepers, and picking up coins (even little cents) is enough to demonstrate to the universe that you are open to the act of receiving. When you bend down and make an effort to pick money from the ground or floor, you are acting as the custodian of wealth. There is a display of respect and courtesy for money lying on the ground.

Apart from letting the universe know you are open to receiving money, you are also acting as a caretaker for the money you find. I know a lot of people feel self-conscious and embarrassed about picking up coins from the ground or street. Reframe your thoughts. Think about yourself as someone who is giving the money its rightful place.

You are looking after the money. As a conscious, purposeful, and intentional custodian of the cash, you are ensuring that money feels respected and loved. This generates even more appreciation energy, which brings greater wealth and abundance your way.

I also recommend always having a hundred dollar bill in your wallet. The technique finds a mention in Abraham Hicks' book *Ask and It Is Given*. The way it works is that there is always a hundred-dollar note in your wallet or money purse and you are never to spend this hundred-dollar bill. The objective is to experience a feeling of safety and security that there is always money available to you in your wallet whenever you need it. You are mentally spending the money without actually spending it.

The mere knowledge that there is money at your disposal immediately increases a sense of positivity and security where money is concerned. This, in turn, expands your wealth-creation mindset and allows greater prosperity to flow your way.

Each time you find coins on the street or ground, bend down to pick it up and rejoice. Celebrate the act of finding money and being its custodian. You will end up attracting more money!

Secret No. 16:
Light Candles (Energy Experiment)

Lighting candles is a great way to grow your physical and spiritual wealth. You'll not only increase your chances of magnetizing wealth and good fortune, you'll also experience a spiritual high. It elevates your mood, positive spirit, and clear thinking. Besides, the fragrance of candles lends an intensely positive aura to your space. Infuse your space with a spiritual aura by lighting some.

I highly recommend creating an abundance altar. It can be any sacred space that you feel good about or experience a connection with. In effect, you are using it to worship money or the money gods and goddess. Light a candle every morning and evening while praying, meditating, or doing your visualizations. Remember, your soul responds on a deeper level to these energies to activate your money-making potential even further.

Set the atmosphere for your soul and subconscious mind to respond. Pick a candle that has a wonderful, positively energizing fragrance that you can connect with success and prosperity on a deeper level.

An energized green candle is considered best for attracting money, wealth, and prosperity. Green is also the preferred color for conducting money and prosperity spells. Since green symbolizes new beginnings, it can revive your not-so-pleasant financial fortunes and transform it into more positive beginnings.

Here is an example of a money and abundance spell performed using a green candle. Pick a new green candle and generously anoint it with lavender, cinnamon, or any other oil. Lavender is the most popular oil for performing money spells. Ensure you like or feel positive about the fragrance of the oil you use because these spells are all about transferring energy. You will in effect transfer a part of your personal energy into the candle, and it won't be effective if you don't like the oil.

Take a paper and mention your desire for more money, prosperity, and good fortune on it. Be fully focused on your heart's deepest desires. Now, light the candle and simply visualize that your desires and wishes are being manifested. Imagine how it'll be to have what you want. Focus on the flame of the green candle to hold your thoughts. Ensure your mind is free from distractions, disturbing thoughts, and self-limiting belief or ideas. You should completely believe in your ability to manifest wealth and abundance with the right intention for the technique to work.

Once you are done visualizing your desires, fold the paper and put it into the candle flames. Watch it light up. Allow it to be collected on an ashtray or vessel. Don't put off the fire; just allow it to continue burning naturally. Most money spells are conducted on Thursdays as they are believed to be the most auspicious days for attracting abundance, wealth, and prosperity.

Another popular spell involves the use of a couple of candles. One is a green candle while the other is metallic gold. The spell has to be done during the waning moon period on a Thursday. To begin, energize both candles. Apply money oil generously on it as you visualize a part of your own energy being transmitted to these candles. Later, carve the words "money" and "prosperity" on the candles. Now, shut your eyes and focus on the visualization. Visualize yourself being wealthy, rich, and fortunate. Pray to the candles to help you magnetize wealth. Finally, snuff the candles.

Secret No. 17:
Obstructions

One of the biggest obstacles to the process of any spiritual attraction is eliminating negative, self-limiting thoughts. A mentally, spiritually, and psychologically healthy individual can place their intention into anything they desire and accomplish the outcome quickly and in a hassle-free manner.

If you consistently place your intention into the abundance, wealth, and lifestyle you desire, you will increase your chances of attracting it.

Are your thoughts in alignment with what you expect? What are the exact thoughts, beliefs, and emotions you expect while focusing on your desires?

Doubts, uncertainty, negative expectations, hopelessness, and low self-esteem end up blocking the flow of your spiritual energy. It is important to clear personal challenges if you truly want to attract more wealth and abundance in your life.

What does a mechanic do when you take your car to him or her? They won't immediately look for ways to boost the performance of your vehicle. Their top priority will be to find out what's wrong with the vehicle and take measures to rectify it.

Take the same approach when it comes to attracting more wealth in your life. Do you have any negative or self-limiting beliefs about money that are blocking your path to wealth and abundance? Identify these self-limiting beliefs and work to eliminate them. If you share an unhealthy relationship with money or view it in a negative light, work to change your perspective about money. If you see it as the root cause of all evil or think all wealthy people are bad, change your view.

Also, feelings of jealousy about other people's wealth and good fortune will seldom help you attract more money. Be genuinely happy for others. Believe that you will also be a recipient of their good fortune. Be happy for and cheer on other people's success. Feel joy in their joy. This way, you are transmitting positive energies about other people's success and money, which will in turn impact your own success, abundance, and good fortune.

Secret No. 18:
Clarity

If you want to increase your chances of manifesting your dreams, be crystal clear about what you want. The universal or spiritual forces, or anything else you like to call them, are *not* known for dealing with mixed or ambiguous messages. When you don't have a clear vision of what you seek, you reduce your chances of manifesting it. If you want stellar results, be precise about what you desire. The universe responds brilliantly to exact wishes and desires! Similarly, avoid changing your mind about what you seek from time to time. It sends the universe on a wild goose chase and doesn't help you manifest your heart's desires.

Think of it like this. What do you do when you order from a catalog? What if you just say you want something blue and big? Or if you end up returning an illegibly filled order form? How about an order form written with multiple confusing requests? You will either end up receiving something you didn't want or nothing at all.

The universe has a catalog of wishes. If you don't point to the exact image and simply offer vague descriptions about what you want, it will get confused. Again, if you keep sending it conflicting, confusing, and vague images about what you want, you are less likely to manifest your desires. Clarify your money, wealth, and abundance goals before you expect to receive from the universe.

What exactly do you seek to accomplish in the next month, six months, or year where monetary or wealth goals are concerned? What car (exact brand, model number, color, etc.) do you wish to own in the coming year? How does your dream house look? What is its entrance, interiors, windows, doors, furnishings, furniture, decorations, kitchen, bathroom, bedrooms, curtains, paintings, beds, floors, walls, and gadgets like? Yes, you've got to be that specific.

179

You'll be blown by accounts of people who visualize their dream house in graphic details (including the colors of its walls and the hardware) and get exactly what they visualized. Start being as detailed and precise about your dreams and visions as you can!

Secret No. 19:
Intention Box (Energy Experiment)

Our words and phrases have magic—that is why it's called *spell*ing, isn't it? Writing about your intentions while focusing all your positive energy is a great way to manifest them. You already have a vision board in place. The next energy experiment to compliment it is to create a wealth intention box.

Begin with a beautiful and meaningful box. You can buy one, but I always recommend creating one to establish a more personal connection with it. This is also a wonderful project to undertake as a family. Next, mention your intentions on individual pieces of post-its. The intention can be any wealth, money, and prosperity-related goal. You may want to increase your company profits or desire a pay hike or earn more passive income.

Ensure that you utilize only positive words and terms while avoiding negative words and terms such as "no" or "not." "I don't want to be in debt" can be reframed as "I want to be financially free." After each intention, write something like "Grant me this or something even better Universe."

With this statement, you are stating that you are open to receiving limitless unexpected opportunities and possibilities. This box can be updated every few weeks or months on new moon days, which are known to have powerful creativity and wish-fulfilling energy. This is a fun and enjoyable way to put the law of attraction into practice and see what you end up manifesting.

Secret No. 20:
Gratitude Jar
(Energy Experiment)

We saw in an earlier chapter how gratitude has increased vibrational energy. A gratitude-filled heart thus becomes a magnet for miracles. When we are grateful for what we currently have, we multiply our blessings. Our energy vibrations instantly rise and become a creation match at all levels. A gratitude jar is a more spiritual experiment that consciously expresses gratitude for each day. This is another individual or family money-manifestation experience designed to multiply your blessings.

Begin with a big jar and prominently put a "gratitude" label on it. You can decorate or beautify the jar as you desire for a more personalized connection. Every day on a tiny piece of paper, mention something your money could buy or something you already have that you are truly grateful for.

When the gratitude jar is full, review everything you are thankful for during the week or month. This one practice is capable of changing your entire life. It aligns you with a positive energy and completely changes your perspective from lack of to limitless and genuine appreciation. It is one of the best ways to activate your money and wealth energy not only to draw new blessings but also to multiply what you currently have.

Secret No. 21:
Mr. Money
(Energy Experiment)

This is another simple yet effective money-manifestation experiment. Begin by imagining Money as a person—a real individual with feelings, emotions, and energies. Create a vision of Money's persona if you like. What does Money look like? Is it a man with grey eyes and a red cloak? Or is it a woman with blue eyes and a black coat? Be as detailed as possible.

Now, write a letter to Mr. or Ms. Money. Tell Money all that you thought about him or her. Pour your heart out about your relationship with each other, perhaps about how he or she had kept you away from a toy you desperately wanted as a child, how you disliked him or her for not being able to buy the dress for your school function, or how you always wanted Money yet he or she was never

185

around. Write about your relationship with money going back to your childhood.

Often, our negative view of money or the unhealthy relation we share with it is directly responsible for our inability to attract wealth and abundance. When you freely express your feelings about money, you release all the pent-up negativity to establish a fresher and more positive bond. This change in your relationship or equation with money helps you pass on the right energies to receive wealth and abundance.

Once you've expressed your true feelings about money, it is easier to realign your feelings and energies about money, which will make you more receptive to it. You'll start sharing a healthier relationship with it, and this will help you attract even more.

After expressing your inherent and deeply held negative beliefs about money, start writing love letters to money. Tell Mr. or Ms. Money how much you adore and appreciate its presence in your life.

Tell Money how thankful you are for the wonderful things it helps you buy or the ways through which it changes your life. Address Money as your confidante—as an ally who helps you accomplish your goals.

Keep doing this money experiment over a period of time and you'll begin noticing the changes in the way wealth responds to you.

Bonus Secret:
Manifestation Technique
(Energy Experiment)

Some folks, despite studying everything about manifestation, struggle to create the material and spiritual wealth they want because they lack intention or a consistent routine. Here is a 7-day manifestation technique that helps with intention setting, being consistent, and silencing all the noise around you.

People often complain that they are overwhelmed by the noise outside them—that they don't get time to complete tasks or even focus on what they want! At times, we are so busy working that there isn't much time to manifest our innermost dreams and desires. Sounds familiar?

The reality is that we are often focusing so much on our outer world or our immediate environment (which consumes a majority of our attention, intention, and energy) that we are left wondering why we don't get what we truly desire.

Let's say you print an article on a piece of paper. You find some mistakes and whiten it. Then, you reprint it. However, the mistake still stays. How? Well, you'll have to make changes to the digital copy, not the outer paper copy. We can't modify our outer world until we bring about changes in our inner world. Everything originates from within. Everything you've manifested or plan to manifest originates from inside you.

Start afresh from within: do this 7-day wealth-manifestation experiment.

1. Pick any three money or wealth related goals that you want to manifest over the next 7 days. It could be a new project or getting money from a deal or simply earning more wage during the week.
2. Next, visualize each desire or goal as if it has already been fulfilled or granted to you.

3. Lastly, mention your results when thanking the universe and acknowledging yourself as a strong creator of your destiny. If you want greater accountability for following these steps or sharing it with the world, I'd recommend writing a blog to track your manifestation success.

Bonus Secret:
Intention Technique
(Energy Experiment)

This simple yet highly effective experiment demonstrates how you impact the world and how you can magnetize your goals and desires based on thoughts, beliefs, feelings, and expectations. The world surrounding you reflects on your beliefs, feelings, and expectations. You come across what you really want to see.

This experiment will demonstrate how your intentions rule what you see and how you experience around the world. It proves that you will find what you genuinely seek or look for and, ultimately, that you can manifest or find anything you seek. It will help you realize that no matter how unrealistic or impractical your current wealth goals appear to be, with the right intention, you can manifest just about anything.

1. In the next 72 hours, actively look for a single specific item. You can use anything from purple cars to bluebirds to bird feathers to a brown horse to pink boxes—just pick something specific.

2. Make an intention of spotting your red boxes or brown horses in the next 72 hours. "I genuinely and truly intend to see brown horses in the next 72 hours."

3. Now, closely watch out for all the brown horses you come across in the next 72 hours. Make a note each time you spot one. You don't have to see physical brown horses. They can be visuals in a magazine or pictures on your social media feed. It could be a pattern on a shirt. Actively watch out for the brown horse imagery. Record your results in a journal or a blog.

4. You'll find yourself coming across more brown horses than usual because you are operating with powerful intention energy.

This will work the same way for the process of money-making and wealth creation.

Conclusion

Thank you for downloading this book and reading through the end. I sincerely hope you enjoyed it and were able to take away several proven strategies for increasing your chances of manifesting wealth, prosperity, and abundance and lead the life of your dreams. Remember, you are in charge of your money and prosperity destiny, and the key to unlocking or activating your money-making powers is within you alone.

I've included lots of real-life examples, practical wisdom, actionable tips, and to-do nuggets to help boost your chances of unlocking or activating powerful principles of wealth manifestation right away. However, you won't accomplish the life of your dreams simply by reading about the power metaphysical principles described in the book. Knowledge without application is futile!

Start implementing the techniques and methods mentioned in the book to unravel your true glorious destiny. Bring about a shift in your mindset and the way you view money to experience a complete transformation in your fortunes. Similarly, take action towards fulfilling your financial goals on a daily basis.

You can't just manifest money by sitting and visualizing money falling into your lap. The law of attraction has to be backed by concrete action if you truly want to manifest your goals.

Finally, if you enjoyed reading the book, please take some time to share your views and post a review. It'd be highly appreciated.

Here's to accomplishing all your goals and leading a wealthy, financially rewarding, and meaningful spiritual life of your dreams!

THE POWER OF METAPHYSICS

A 27-Day Journey To A New Life

Introduction

In an old parable, a wise old farmer stepped outside of his home to take in the evening air. Looking out toward the horizon, he gazed at a magnificent moon. As he admired the moon, his grandson came out to join him. The two chatted for a while when his grandson asked him the following question. "Grandpa, what is the secret to becoming happy?" The farmer whistled for his dog to come, which ran right over. The farmer pointed his finger at the moon. In reaction to the farmer's gesture, the dog fixated his gaze on the farmer's finger.

The farmer turned to his grandson and replied: "I was pointing to a magnificent moon, but my dog placed its focus on my finger." Most of us behave like the dog in the parable. We have placed our focus on what we believe points to happiness rather than experiencing happiness as it naturally exists.

There has never been a person who has not sought happiness. We may not be consciously seeking happiness; however, we are doing so subconsciously. The pursuit of happiness is hardwired within us. Even a person who takes their own life does so because they feel that it would be less painful than living. To borrow from a famous song, we are looking for happiness in all the wrong places.

Just as the farmer's dog, we are fixated on finding happiness by focusing on objects while being unaware of its source. What are the objects that we focus on in our pursuit of happiness? The list is endless. The more popular ones are relationships, sex, money, our careers, status, power, alcohol, drugs, the approval of others, and so on. In fact, anything that you can think, see, hear, touch, or taste, is an object and can become the object of our focus. Anything that you can conceptualize in your mind or detect with your senses is considered phenomenal. Since we experience the world phenomenally, this is where most of us have sought out our happiness.

True happiness and freedom occur when we shift our attention from that which seems to point to happiness and start focusing the nature of happiness itself. In order focus on the nature of happiness, we first need focus on the nature of who we are. It is by taking on the endless journey into the self that all that we could desire is revealed to us.

This book is about learning to shift your perspective. It is by shifting your perspective from the world of objects to the nature of awareness that you will be able to partake in the endless journey into the self. To assist you in this journey, this book is divided into five chapters, with each chapter dedicated to a specific core principle in metaphysics. In turn, each chapter represents a week of practices that you can easily apply in your daily life. By the end of this book, you will have developed a basic foundation for changing the trajectory of your life. Are you ready to stop focusing on the pointers in our life and start to gazing at the magnificent moon that is your truth?

Week 1

Λ

The Silent Discovery: Why Silence is the greatest Teaching

Imagine that you are walking into a forest, and you come across a small pond. You throw a small rock into the pond and then look into it. Your reflection in its waters is distorted by the ripples from the splash. After a few minutes, the ripples disappear and leave the water surface as smooth as glass. This time when you look into the pond you see a clear image of yourself. Not only do you see a clear image of yourself, you see a clear image of everything around you, the trees, the mountains, and the sky.

For most of us, our experience of life is like the pond with ripples. We never clearly see into the nature of life, or of ourselves, because of the distortion that we experience. The distortion I speak of are the ripples of illusions that are created when lack clarity in how we perceive our essential nature.

We have clarity of our essential nature because we have lost the silence within us, the silence which is our direct connection with the essence of who we are. The good news is that the silence that I speak of never was lost, to lose it is impossible. Rather, we have forgotten about it due to our fixation on objects.

We have forgotten about silence because we have been socialized to experience life as being something outside ourselves. This socialization goes back for innumerable generations. Because we have divorced ourselves from our essential self, we have become fixated with the objects of our lives. We have allowed these objects to define our sense of self and the quality of our lives.

Both silence and objects are inherent aspects of life. In fact, silence is also an object. I will address this point later on in the book. For now, we will discuss the significance of silence. The silence that we will be discovering has nothing to do with any sounds that may be in your environment. The silence that I speak of is the stillness that is within you.

Day 1

Challenging Perception

We will start off with a simple exercise that can facilitate the experiencing of silence and the nature of awareness (note: This exercise may take practice before you experience its effect).

1. Sit down, make yourself comfortable.
2. Place your awareness on an object within your environment. I want you to observe this object, making it the point of your focus.
3. If I asked you to report back to me of what you know about the object, what would you tell me?

I would guess that you would tell me the name of the object, a description of what it looks like, and perhaps what the object was doing. For example, if the object that I was looking at was a tree, I could tell you of its appearance, its color, its height, and the shape of its leaves. I may even be able to tell you the species that the tree belongs to and where this species of tree is found.

Now that I have given you my example, take a look at your object again. What is it that you know about your object?

Now that you have finished with this exercise, we are ready to bring our discussion back to silence. If you are like most of humanity, your report back to me would be comprised of facts and opinions about your object. Your report back to me might be stated in one sentence, or you may be able to give an extensive account of your experience. Regardless of what you report back, you will most likely believe the findings of your observation are an accurate account of your object. We will now take the last exercise and break it down to challenge your experience of observing.

1. Look at your object again. How is it that you know the size of your object, its color, or any other information that you see? Most likely, you would reply back "Because I saw it."

2. Take another look at your object. Determine for yourself if you can separate the seeing of the object from the object itself. In other words, can I separate my seeing of the tree from the tree itself? Put another way, is there a point where seeing stops and your object begins or do the act of seeing and your object merge into each other? I hope that you will realize that the act of seeing and the object being seen are inseparable from each other.

3. Assuming that you agree with me that the seeing of your object is dependent on the existence of the object itself, my next question to you is how do you know that seeing is taking place? You know that the act of seeing is taking place because you are aware of it. You have awareness that seeing is taking place.

4. Now, look at your object again. Can you separate the awareness of the seeing from the act of seeing? This question may be more difficult than the last question, so take your

time to determine this for yourself. Eventually, you will realize that the awareness of seeing and the act of seeing are also one in the same.

Let us summarize what we have just discovered:

- The seeing of the object and the object itself are one in the same.
- The awareness of the act of seeing and the act of seeing itself are also one in the same.

We can conclude from these realizations that nothing exists apart from awareness, that awareness and that which is known are inseparable from each other. If you were able to experience that which I was guiding you toward in this exercise, look at your object again from this new perspective. Do you feel differently about your experience of seeing? Does it change what you can tell me about your object?

Before you first did this exercise, your first observation of the object was like the pond that just had the rock thrown into it. Like the ripples of the pond, your thoughts distorted any deeper experience of your object that you could have potentially experienced.

As you practice this exercise, using the guidance that I offered, the ripples that are created by your mind's activities will gradually diminish. Just like the still water of the pond, your experience of life will be clearer, more unified. The previous exercise can also be adjusted to apply to remaining four senses.

Silence, also known as stillness, is the ability not to get caught up in our mind's chatter and to be able to discern the subtleties of reality that reflect its essential nature. You cannot know anything about that which you experience; you can only have a knowing (awareness) of the existence of experience.

I cannot know anything about a tree. I can only know of my perceptions of the tree. I can know of the sensations that I feel when I touch the tree, and I can know of the sounds of its leaves rustling in the wind. I can also know of my thoughts of the tree, but I cannot know the tree itself. When awareness illuminates experience, without being distorted by our thinking, the secrets of the universe will reveal themselves as effortlessly as the reflections of still water. This is the power of silence.

Daily Exercise:

The exercise that you did in this section normally needs to be practiced before you can experience a notable change in how you perceive reality. Continue practice this exercise.

Day 2

The Nature of the Mind

There is a story of a servant whose master lived in a large mansion. The strange thing was the relationship that the servant had with his master in that the servant had never seen him! The master never ventured from his room, and all communication occurred through the closed door of the master's bedroom. If the master needed something, he would signal the servant who would come to his closed door to receive his orders.

One day, the servant was telling his friend about his frustration that he was experiencing with his master. He shared with his friend that his master was never satisfied, that he was always finding fault with him. His master was always demanding more from him. His friend suggested that he should discuss his concerns with his master. His friend's advice rang true for him. He needed to tell his master how he felt. Gathering his courage, he went to his master's room and knocked on the door. To his surprise, his master did not respond. He knocked a second time, still no response. The servant began to worry. Could it be that his master was in trouble?

The servant gathered his nerve and reached for the doorknob. To his shock, the door was unlocked! When he opened the door, he was left speechless. The room was empty! There was not master, no furniture, no carpet, no curtains; there was nothing! The servant sunk into despair. He realized that he had spent his life serving a master that did not exist!

The story that you just read is a metaphor for the relationship that most of us have with our minds. The servant symbolizes you and me; the master represents our minds. Just like the servant, most of us live out our lives obeying our minds. Just like the master, our minds are constantly making demands of us and are never satisfied. All problems that we experience, both at the individual and collective level, are the result of our unquestioned allegiance to our minds.

My hope for you is that by applying the core metaphysical principles that are found in this book, you will gradually experience a shift in your relationship with your mind. Instead of your mind being in charge of you, you will take charge of your mind. Instead of a being a tyrant who is always demanding more from you, your mind will serve you as a tool for us solve problems, creating new possibilities, and explore higher levels of consciousness.

In the last section, you performed exercises that invited you to inquire into the subtleties of observing an object. The mind operates at the conceptual level. In other words, the mind can only detect those things that can be discerned by the senses or conceived as a concept by the mind. Those things in our experience that possess these qualities are considered to be phenomenal. That which can be perceived through our senses is registered by the mind. The mind operates by creating conceptual representations of the information that it obtains from our senses. When I look at a tree, my eyes take in visual information about the tree and convert into electric impulses by way of the optic nerve. When the electric impulses reach the brain, it descrambles the digitized information and reassembles it into a conceptual image of the tree.

Whenever we experience anything conceptually, we perceive an image created by the mind, rather than perceiving the truth of its existence. The "tree" that I see in my backyard is not the true reality. The "tree" that I experience is a conceptual image in my mind that I believe is the actual tree. It is for this reason that I made the statement the last section that we can never know anything about our experiences; we can only know of experience. The only thing that I can know about a tree is my knowing of its conceptual image.

Regarding the exercises from the previous section, if you were able to experience how the awareness of an object and the object itself are indivisible, then you had a most profound discovery that eludes the majority of humanity. That fact that most of humanity has not had this experience leads to the understanding why true freedom remains just an idealistic notion for most of us. The achievement of true freedom is independent of the conditions of our lives. There are people in prison who enjoy greater freedom than some multi-millionaires. The experience of true freedom is the product of mastering our relationship with our minds.

There is not one problem that a human being can experience that is not the result of a limited sense of self. At the deepest level, the root of all actions or behaviors is thought. Everything that we do originates from thought. Essentially, there are only two kinds of thoughts, fearful and loving. Thoughts of fear are based on a sense of separation, that we are separate from the rest of life. Thoughts of love arise from a sense of connection, from a sense of an oneness with life. Sincere, loving thoughts remove our sense of separation, fear does not exist. It is difficult for us not to feel separate from life when most of us experience life through the concepts that we create of it.

Imagine that you go to the Grand Canyon and come across the most amazing scenic view of the canyon's majesty. You witness the beautifully rugged canyon walls, the amazing rock formations, and its raging waters. You are so impressed with what you see that you decide to take a picture of it using a cheap disposable camera. When you look at the developed picture, you realize that it no way does the picture come even close to that which you experienced. Similarly, our concepts are like the photograph. They are a poor representation of the infinite grandeur that is life.

Most of us experience life through our concepts of it. In fact, our sense of self is also a concept. The reason why most of us are servants to our minds is that we believe in the concepts that are our minds create, including our sense of self.

Here is a simple exercise. Answer this question: Who are you? When most people are asked this question, they come up with responses (if they can come up with a response at all) such as:

- I am a man
- I am a woman
- I am undeserving
- I am a good person.
- I am shy.
- I am a rebel.
- I am a parent.
- I am a teacher.
- I am a winner.
- I am a human being.
- I am a citizen of the planet.

Regardless of how you answer this question, you are using concepts to define who you are. We have identified ourselves with concepts because we have personalized our experience of it. We experience ourselves based on what our mind tells us. It is only through silence that we can transcend our concepts and experience for ourselves that aspect of ourselves that is more fundamental than anything that the mind can grasp. To transcend our minds is to change our relationship with it. When we transcend our mind, we become like the servant who found out that his master's room was empty.

Day 3

Perceiving the Illusions of Reality

So far in this chapter, we explored inner silence and the nature of the mind. We also discussed how we focus on objects, which make up the phenomenal world. We discussed that the phenomenal world includes everything that we can detect with our minds or senses. Most of us live out our lives from the phenomenal perspective. In other words, our awareness is limited to the world of form.

Because our focus is on the world of form, we have come to identify with the world form. How we define ourselves, how we experience ourselves, is often determined by the phenomenal. Here is an example:

Joe is driving his car to work when he gets cut off by another driver, who is not paying attention. Joe experiences anger and curses the other driver. When he arrives at work, Joe is informed by his boss that he will be getting a bonus. Hearing this news, Joe is happy. Later that day, Joe gets a call from a difficult client. Joe becomes frustrated. At the end of the day, Joe arrives home and is embraced by his family. Now, Joe feels loved and supported.

Through his day, Joe experienced a wide range of emotional states, and each state caused Joe to experience himself differently. Further, he believed that the changes to his emotional state were due to the situations that he encountered. He attributes these changes to the other driver, the bonus, the difficult client, and his family. Joe is an example of how our sense of self is shaped by the situations and events of our lives. Because change is a constant in life, our sense of self is unstable. One moment we can feel like that we are on the top of the world, only to feel defeated when the winds of change blow by us.

Now consider your own life. What has changed in your life since you were a young child? Have your thoughts changed? Have your beliefs changed? Have your relationships changed? Has your body changed? Has your experience of the world changed? Has the way you see yourself changed? Everything that you have ever experienced has changed at some level. Nothing in life remains static or constant, at least at the phenomenal level.

For us to say that everything in life changes; however, it not enough. How do you know change is occurring? You know that change is occurring the same way you knew of the object in the previous exercise. You know of change because you are aware of it. However, for you to be aware of change, you need to be aware of that which does not change. How can you know anything without knowing the opposite? How can you know cold unless you also know hot? How can you know calm unless you also know anger?

There is an aspect of you that is aware of change, including the changes that you undergo physically, mentally, and emotionally. The reason why this aspect of you is aware of change is that it is changeless. Only that which is changeless can perceive that which changes. How else could change be known? There is an aspect of you that exists within the silence of your being and is beyond any concept. The aspect that I speak of cannot be comprehended by the mind, for this non-phenomenal. To say something is non-phenomenal is to say that it cannot be detected by the senses or conceived by the mind.

What we refer to as "reality" is the unfolding of life, an unfolding that is witnessed by your non-phenomenal self. There is no true reality; rather, what we refer to as reality is the constantly changing projection of consciousness. The illusions of reality are that we live in a physical world, of which we are a separate entity. We see ourselves as being separate from other people, other objects, and from our environment. Because we experience ourselves as being separate, we pursue the objects of the physical realm in the belief that they will make us happy and free us from our sufferings.

Because nothing in the phenomenal world is permanent, we experience a sense of loss or disappointment when things change. We are like a hamster on the wheel. No matter how fast we run, we never get to where we want to be, that place where lasting peace exists. We have fallen for the illusions of reality, that there is something out there that will give us what we want to experience.

Ultimate peace comes from establishing ourselves in the unchanging while enjoying the experience of the changing. The unchanging is your essential being. That which changes is the myriad expressions of your essential being. That which you experience as being you is the form that your essential being used to experiences the myriad expressions of itself. It was stated earlier that awareness of experience and experience itself are inseparable. Your essential being is awareness, and all that you are aware of is experience. Because awareness cannot be separate from experience, you are one with all that is.

Daily Exercise:

Here is an exercise for developing your ability to perceive without conceptualizing your experience:

1. Sit down and view your surroundings, taking your time to take everything in.

2. When you are ready, close your eyes and allow yourself to relax.

3. Imagine that you are an alien from a distant planet who has arrived on Earth to study it. You have no information about this planet, nor do you have any past experience to draw from. Because of this, you are unable to define, identify, analyze, or judge anything that you experience. In other words, you are a blank slate.

4. No open your eyes and look at your surroundings again. Take your time.

5. How did your experience observing compare with your first observation?

If you did not notice any difference between the two observations, practice this exercise until you do. Anytime we incorporate our thoughts or judgments while observing, we perceive things conceptually. To be able to observe without utilizing conceptual thinking is part of being mindful and present.

Day 4

Phenomenal vs. Non-Phenomenal

In this chapter, there has been frequent reference to the terms phenomenal and non-phenomenal. To quickly review, phenomenal refers to anything that you can experience directly. Everything that we know about our world is phenomenal. Anything that exists beyond our ability to perceive is non-phenomenal. Our minds function conceptually, meaning that information that is received by the mind is converted into a concept.

Words and images are an example of conceptual constructs of the mind. Words and images are solely the product of the mind. Without the mind, images and words would not exist. We do not "see" images. As indicated before, our eyes take in visual information, which is converted to electrical impulses. The electrical impulses are then converted into images by the brain. Similarly, words are linguistic constructions of the mind that are used to convey a thought. You may wonder why I switch from using "mind" to "brain." For now, I am writing this way purely for reasons of semantics. We will discuss later the difference between the mind and the brain.

If images are the products of the information that is gathered by sight, and words are the mind's representation of thought, where does information and thought come from? Thought and information are one in the same. What we call thought is information that is perceived by consciousness. At the most fundamental, everything that exists is information. However, we can go one step further. Information is a form of energy. Everything that exists is an expression of energy. However, this energy is not the kind of energy that we experience in our daily lives. The kind of energy I am speaking of is not electrical. The energy that I speak of is aware of itself. The energy that I am speaking of is consciousness.

In the first section of this book, you did an exercise where you observed an object. In doing this exercise, you hopefully concluded that it is impossible to separate the awareness of an object with the object itself. Awareness and consciousness are just two different terms for the same thing. The fundamental nature of all that exists is consciousness. Everything that exists arises from consciousness. Without consciousness, there can be no experience.

Going back to the terms non-phenomenal and phenomenal, these are just concepts that our mind uses to explain that which it can perceive and that which it cannot. In truth, words, concepts, mind, this book, and you, are just the physical manifestations of consciousness. At the most basic level, there is no difference between the phenomenal realm and a non-phenomenal realm. There is no difference between spirituality and materialism. There is no difference between reality and fantasy. Finally, there is no difference between you and universe itself. Any sense of difference or distinction is a product of our minds.

There are researchers who are spending countless hours pursuing the origins of the universe or the nature of matter. Their searches will be never-ending. They are chasing concepts when the answers that they are looking for lie in the depths of their own lives.

Daily Exercise:

1. Sit down and allow yourself to relax.
2. Now, look at an object that you are familiar with. Make this object the focus of your attention.
3. When you have familiarized yourself with this object, close your eyes and visualize this object in your mind, to the best of your ability.

Every one visualizes differently, so do not make any judgments about your ability to visualize. Imagine your object to the best of your abilities.

4. When you have the image in your mind, notice the qualities of this image. How does this image appear to you? Is it blurry or clear? Is faint without any distinguishable features or does have it vivid detail? Do the qualities of your image change in intensity or form, or do they remain static?

5. Can you determine where your image appeared from? Can you determine where your image goes when it fades?

6. Now visualize something that is imaginary, something that does not exist in your reality. Perhaps it is a unicorn or a purple elephant.

7. When you have the image in your mind, notice the qualities of this image. How does this image appear to you? Is it blurry or clear? Is faint without any distinguishable features or does have it vivid detail? Do the

qualities of your image change in intensity or form, or do they remain static?

8. Can you determine where your image appeared from? Can you determine where your image goes when it fades?

Is there any difference between your visualization of the imaginary object and the one you that you observed? Can you tell the difference between "reality" and "fantasy"?

Meditation

So far in this first chapter, we have discussed silence, the illusions of the mind, and phenomenal and non-phenomenal existence. Hopefully you have found this discussion interesting; however, everything that you have read so far is just a concept. It has been just food for your mind. Concepts are necessary aspect of being human beings. We are social creatures who need concepts to communicate and exchange ideas. For this purpose, concepts are invaluable.

The same is true of the mind. Our minds are the key to our evolutionary success. The greatest force behind our dominance as a species is the result of our ability to solve problems. The downfall for our species is that we have identified with our minds. We believe that who we are is our minds and bodies.

Our sense of separation, resulting from our identification with our mind and body, has caused us to act out of fear, the fear of scarcity and the fear of loss. It is from this perspective that all our challenges arise from, be they at the individual or collective level. Further, it limits our potential to experience higher levels of consciousness and awareness.

Imagine an actor who is performing in a play. This actor has deeply identified with her character and is flawless in how she presents her character to the audience. When the play is over, she removes her make-up, changes her clothes, and goes home. The actor no longer plays the role of her character. She is now becoming a spouse, a parent, a friend, or a daughter. She may party with her friends, go camping, or go out on a date. What the actor can do off stage is endless.

When we identify with the mind or body, we are like the actor who still believes that she is her character when the play is over. We need to learn how to transcend our minds and experience the deeper and more profound aspects of ourselves. One of the most powerful tools for this purpose is meditation. The heart of meditation is returning to silence. It perceives the illusions of reality, and it connects us with the non-phenomenal realm.

Daily Exercise:

There are some key points to keep in mind when learning how to meditate:

1. Maintain an attitude of total acceptance and non-judgment for everything you experience.
2. Do not try to control, change, or resist anything that you experience.
3. Allow all that you experience the complete freedom to express itself.
4. When meditating, you may experience thoughts such as:

a. My thoughts keep coming; they are not slowing down.
b. This is too difficult.
c. This is boring.
d. I have more important things to do.
e. This is not working.
f. Am I doing this right?

Ignore these thoughts and continue to focus on the meditation.

Finally, there is no correct way or incorrect way to meditate as long as you are allowing yourself to be a witness to all of your experiences.

1. Sit down in a comfortable position, close your eyes, and breathe normally.
2. Place your attention on your breath by focusing on the sensations of it traveling in and out of your body.
3. As your focus on your breath, you experience the appearance of thoughts. When they appear, simply ignore them and return your attention back to your breath.

4. If you keep your focus on your breath, there will come the point when you can maintain your awareness of it without any effort. When you reach this stage, allow yourself to be the witness to all that appears in your awareness.

5. Notice how thoughts, sensations, and perceptions appear in your awareness and then fade away. These mental phenomena appear and disappear in your awareness. However, that which is awareness remains constant and unchanging.

6. The mental phenomena that you experience will have the qualities of being positive, neutral, or negative; yet, awareness itself is untouched by any of these qualities.

7. As you give less importance to the experiencing of mental phenomena, they will lose their energy, and your mind will become calm; you may even experience periods of stillness and space. If you do, know that stillness and space is also a mental

phenomenon. Do not become attached to any experience; rather, remain as a witness to it.

8. Continue to meditate for as long as you desire.

Day 6

The Nature of Experience

Because we identify with our minds and bodies, we experience ourselves as being a separate and unique entity that exists in a world of other entities, both living and non-living. As I sit and write this passage, I am aware of the words that appear on the screen of my laptop. I am also aware of the room that I am in, my wife who is upstairs, and my dog that is lying on the carpet. I am aware of the song that is playing on the radio, and I am aware of myself. Because I experience thoughts and the sensations of my body, I believe that the words, the room that I am in, my wife, my dog, and the song are separate entities that exist outside of me. All these other entities are what are commonly known as "experience."

As we explored in the first section of this chapter, it is impossible to separate the awareness of an experience with the experience itself.

I offer you another exercise so that what I speak of can be directly experienced by you. Direct experience is vital when exploring the metaphysical. Without direct experience, all that we are left with is theory.

Daily Exercise:

This next exercise builds on the exercise from day 1 and will challenge your further in questioning how you perceive reality.

1. Sit in a comfortable place and close your eye, allow yourself to relax.
2. Breathing normally, place your focus on the flow of your breath. Notice the sensations

that you experience as your breath flows in and out of your body.

3. Should you become distracted by thought, simply return your focus to your breath.

4. As you focus on your breath, do not judge any experience that you encounter. Welcome every experience that you have without making any attempts to change or modify it.

5. As you focus on your breath, do not hold any expectations of what should be happening. Do not exert any effort. Allow everything that happens to occur.

6. When you feel calm and relaxed, remove your focus from your breath and place it on your thoughts.

7. Notice that you are aware of your thoughts. As you focus on your thoughts, what happens to them? Do your thoughts change in any way? Do they change in their intensity? Do they seem to appear and fade with time? Where do your thoughts arise from? Where do they go when they fade?

8. Now shift your attention from your thoughts to the sensations that you experience in your body.

9. Notice that you are aware of your sensations. As you focus on your sensations, what happens to them? Do your sensations change in any way? Do they change in their intensity? Do they seem to appear and fade with time? Where do your sensations arise from? Where do they go when they fade?

10. With your eyes closed, reach out and touch something. It could be the object that you are sitting on, your arm or leg, or an object in the room.

11. When you touch the object, ask yourself if you are experiencing the object itself or are experiencing the sensation of the object. Can you separate the sensation of the object from the object itself? Where does this sensation appear from? Where does this sensation go when it fades? Determine the answers to these questions for yourself.

12. Notice that you are aware of the changing of sensation as it comes and goes.

13. Now ask yourself if you can separate the awareness of sensation from the sensation itself.

14. Now open your eyes and look at an object. As you observe the object, ask yourself if you can separate the seeing of the object from seeing itself. Determine the answer to this question for yourself.

15. Ask yourself if you can separate the awareness of seeing from the seeing itself.

16. Close your eyes again, and allow yourself to relax. When you are feeling relaxed, ask yourself is it possible to experience anything without the awareness of it. Determine the answer to this question for yourself.

17. Now ask yourself if it is possible to separate the awareness of experience from experience itself.

I hope that you will discover that awareness and experience are one in the same. This is because experience arises from awareness, also known as consciousness. What we refer to as experience is the phenomenal expression of consciousness, which is non-phenomenal. When this is understood, you will know intuitively that any sense of separateness is just an illusion that is created by the conceptual mind. From higher perspectives of consciousness, everything is one.

The reason that you were unable to determine the place where thoughts and sensations arise and fade is that they arise and fade from consciousness. The objects that you touched or saw also came from consciousness. Even your sense of existing, of being alive, is an expression of consciousness. Your sense of being aware arises from consciousness. That who you believe to be arises from consciousness.

There is a reason why you experience yourself as having a physical body, and that reason is that having a physical allows you to experience the phenomenal world. It was stated earlier in this book that the fundamental aspect of the universe is energy and energy that is aware. That energy is consciousness and consciousness is constantly expanding through the gaining of information. Information can only be gained through experience. Since consciousness is non-phenomenal, it cannot experience anything other than itself. In other words, awareness can only know awareness. To gain information it needs to manifest as phenomenal objects (like you and me) so that it can have an experience. It is through experience that information is gained.

Whenever you have an experience, you are informing the pure consciousness (from which you manifested from) of that experience through the information that you gained from it. The information which we gain from experience is thought.

Thought provides consciousness with information that it can use to expand and create new manifestations, which are consistent with the information that it received. What is commonly known as the Law of Attraction is this process that the pure consciousness is constantly performing.

Day 7

The Psychological Self

The idea that we are phenomenal expressions of a larger consciousness can be difficult to comprehend because we experience the world at a conceptual level. It requires the transcendence of our normal consciousness awareness for this idea to become self-evident. Luckily, most of us experience this transcendence when we go to bed at night.

When you dream at night, you take on an altered state of consciousness. In the unfolding of your dream, you experience yourself in the dream as your dream self. Your dream self has thoughts, feelings, and perceptions of the dream world that it finds itself in. It can make decision, plan, anticipate, and take action as it engages with its dream world. As real as your dream may seem, while it is occurring, both your dream self and its dream world are the projections of your sleeping self. Similarly, your experience of being a separate and unique being, in your waking life, is also a projection of pure consciousness.

When we awake from a dream, it becomes evident to us that the dream self that we experienced was just a psychological manifestation of ourselves. The reason why our dream self, and its dream experience, was so real for us is that consciousness identified with it. The reason why consciousness identified with it was that our dream was based on thoughts that were meaningful to us. Similarly, you identify with your mind and body because the thoughts and beliefs that you hold of your mind and body are meaningful to you as well.

Your dream self is a psychological self that you experience while sleeping just as your waking self is the psychological self that is the projection of the pure consciousness. There is, however, a stage of consciousness where we transcend our psychological self.

Unlike dream sleep, we are free of thought in a deep sleep. Deep sleep is pure consciousness. When we enter deep sleep, pure consciousness removes its awareness from the world of objects (which includes thoughts) and redirects its attention toward itself. In a deep sleep, awareness is observing awareness.

Because deep sleep is devoid of thought, we have no memory of it. To have a memory requires experience, which deep sleep is devoid of. When we wake up in the morning, we are aware that we experienced deep sleep, but we have no recollection of the experience of it. Further, in a deep sleep, we lose all experience of ourselves. The reason why we felt rejuvenated and vitalized after waking from deep sleep is that we forgot about our existence as a person. We forgot about our existence as a person because our essential self was reunited with itself.

Daily Exercise:

This next exercise involves self-inquiry as you explore the nature of that which you refer to as "you." When performing this exercise, it is critical that you do not rely on what you believe that you know. Instead, I want to rely purely on your direct experiences as you perform this exercise. Do not go by what you think; go by what you experience. Also, I recommend that you read through this meditation first before practicing it. Or, record it on audio tape and play it back as you do this exercise.

1. When answering this question, do not rely on your thinking. You will not get an answer.

2. Sit down in a comfortable position and close your eyes.

3. Allow yourself to follow your breath during inhalation and exhalation. Place your

attention on your breath. Feel it as it courses through your body.

4. Take on an attitude of complete allowing, that whatever arises during this meditation you will have complete acceptance of it.

5. Observe the perceptions, thoughts, sensations, feelings, and emotions that arise within you. Allow them to come and go on their own accord. All you need to do is be the observer of them.

6. You are the observer of thought, sensation, perception, emotions, and feeling. You are the one that is aware of experience. But who are you? You refer to yourself as "I," but who is this "I"?

7. Where is this "I"? Can you find where this "I" is located? Is it located in your body? Is it located in your heart?

8. The word "phenomenal" means something that can be seen, thought of, touched, heard, or detected somehow.

9. As you search for the location of "I," know that whatever you encounter is phenomenal in nature.

10. Anything you experience is phenomenal, everything you know is phenomenal.

11. Even if you experience space, a sense of emptiness, or bliss, this is not who you are. Space, emptiness, and bliss are also phenomenal because they can be detected by you.

12. Are you phenomenal? Everything that is phenomenal is subject to change. Your thoughts, sensations, feelings, and emotions are constantly changing.

13. Your thoughts come in and out of awareness? Who is observing thought coming in and out of awareness? Are you coming in and out of awareness?

14. Your emotions and feelings are constantly changing? Are you constantly changing?

15. No matter what your response is to these questions, there is awareness of your response. What is aware of your response?

16. The essence of who you are does not change; it is eternal.

17. Who you are cannot be observed; it cannot be felt, and it cannot be detected. Who you are is not phenomenal.

18. Who you are cannot be experienced. Who you are is awareness itself. Just as a ray of

light cannot shine on itself, the awareness that is you cannot observe itself. You have a knowing that you exist.

19. The more you discover that which you are not, the closer you will come to realizing who you are.

20. This is the end of this meditation. Allow yourself to remain in silence for as long as you desire.

Week 2

The Power of Thoughts and Beliefs:
How the Mind creates Reality

If we use the analogy of a computer, thoughts are units of information just as bits are units of information for a computer. Because we identify with our minds and bodies, we believe that we are the creator's of thought, that the thoughts that we have belong to us. Just as your dream self appears to think during the course of the dream, your psychological self also appears to be thinking.

At the most fundamental level, everything is one. What we interpret to be "our thoughts" is really our manifested self attracting thoughts that are consistent with the level of consciousness that we have reached. Every living being is tapping into the collective consciousness and attracting the information that is consistent with its conscious awareness. Sometimes referred to as the Akashi Records, the collective consciousness contains every thought that has ever, or will ever, be thought.

The greater consciousness system refers to all aspects of consciousness. It includes pure consciousness, all manifestations of pure consciousness, and the localized consciousness that is experienced by each manifested expression of consciousness.

It is the nature of pure consciousness to seek expansion as well as to support the success and happiness of each of its manifestation. In carrying out these functions, the pure consciousness employs thought.

Thought is the information that is generated by experience, which informs all aspects of the greater consciousness system. Further, it is the informing of the various components of the larger consciousness system that leads to the expansion of consciousness, both of pure consciousness and that of its localized expressions. Here is an example of how this process works:

A child (a manifestation of consciousness that experiences localized consciousness) is trying to figure out how to solve a math problem. The child's attempts do not lead to the resolving of the problem. The child's attempts are guided by thought, the thought that he or she attracted.

If the thoughts lead to actions that do not solve the desired outcome, an experience of contrast occurs. In this case, the contrast is the result of the desired outcome (the resolution of the problem) and what the child experiences, the problem remains unsolved. The experience of contrast leads to the greater consciousness to manifesting other phenomena that are consistent with the child's desired outcome. As a result, the child gains access to thoughts of how to solve the problem that it did not consider before. The child changes their approach to solving the problem until the problem is solved. The flow of information (thought) is what leads to the expansion of localized consciousness (the child) and that of pure consciousness.

Thought is the conceptual representation of consciousness's infinite potential for expression. Because of our conceptual mind, we are unable to experience the infinite potential of consciousness, so the thoughts that we attract are like a snapshot of that infinite intelligence. To better understand this, it is like comparing a single frame with the full-length movie that it came from. Most of us are at the conscious level where we can only detect a single frame. The higher the level of conscious awareness that we achieve the more of the movie we can experience.

The ultimate purpose of studying metaphysics is to apply the teachings to our lives so that we can expand our awareness. The greater the expansion of awareness, the closer we come to realizing the truth of our own existence.

While thoughts are bits of information, beliefs are those thoughts that we take to be true. Beliefs are those thoughts of which we have developed a great sense of certainty for. Referring back to the movie metaphor, holding onto a belief is like us seeing a single frame of the movie and believing to know the movie's plot.

Because of our sense of certainty in our beliefs, they determine our experience of life. Like tinted sunglasses, beliefs color our experience of the world and ourselves. If I believe that the world is a dangerous place, then that will be my experience of the world. If I believe love is the foundation of life that that will be my experience of life.

Like everything else that is phenomenal, thoughts arise from the non-phenomenal. Further, thoughts are a vital aspect of the manifestation process. The manifestation process occurs in stages and starts off with the manifestation of desire. Desire is the initial and most fundamental manifestation of pure consciousness. Desire then manifest as thought, which contains information that is consistent with desire. In turn, thought manifest as emotions. Emotions manifest into action, and action manifest as physical form. This process is so ingrained in us that we are not even aware of it. Further, we only pay attention to the final stage, which is the actual manifestation. Most of us are unaware of all the stages that lead up to the actual manifestation. Additionally, we take the credit or the blame for the final manifestation.

Imagine a person who faces an obstacle; they need to increase their income because they are unable to make ends meet. The manifestation of a solution to this person's obstacle is desire, the desire to earn more money. Desire than manifest as thought, the thought of what this person can do to change their situation. The thought this person attracts could be the thought of looking for a new job, thoughts of the kind of job that they want, or thoughts of how to manage their money more effectively, and so on.

The thoughts that this person attract then manifest into emotion. Emotion creates the energy to turn thoughts into action. The emotions that this person experiences could be the emotion of fear or frustration for their current situation, or it could be the emotion of passion to make a change in their fiancés. Either way, emotions provide the fuel for change. The pain of financial struggle makes the person want to make a change while passion drives them forward. Emotion then manifest as action: The person searches for employment opportunities, sends out resumes, and develops a budget. With continued focus, action turns into physical form, which may include a new job and more money.

Notice that through our socialization process, which causes us to identify with our mind and body, we put all of our focus on the action component. The actual manifestation, the new job, and more money were a product of all the previous steps. The final step, the step of action, is what activated the inherent power found in each of the previous steps.

Day 8

Values

This week is about transforming your thoughts and beliefs so that they support you by reducing the resistance that you experience within yourself. By reducing your resistance, you improve your alignment with pure consciousness. Day 8 is about identifying your values.

Values are an indicator of what we value in life. Unlike the way values are traditionally thought of, the values that I speak of have to do with states of being or emotional states that we value. For example, a common traditional value would that of family. For our discussion, family is not a value. However, the emotional states that having a family give us is a value. Examples of values include:

- Love

- Compassion
- Contribution
- Security
- Fun
- Transcendence

Anytime we live in a manner that is inconsistent with our values; we create major resistance in our lives. If your life is not aligned with your values, start the process of making changes in your life so that you can start creating greater alignment. If you currently have a job that conflicts with your values, what can you do to create the needed changes in your work? Could you conduct your work differently? Would it require you take on a different position? Perhaps it means finding a new job. If the relationship you are in does not align with your values, what changes do you need to make? Do you need to transform your relationship or find a new one? Take into account any aspect of your life where you experience a gap between the way you live your life and the values that you hold.

The following are examples of creating resistance by going against our values:

- You value passion but do not pursue your dreams out of fear losing the security of the job that you hate.
- You value connection but pending all your time working when rather than being with your family.
- You value personal growth but always do things the same way just because you were taught or raised to believe that it is the way that it should be done.

Daily Exercise:

Create a list of your values and order them according to how important they are to you. You can identify your values by asking the question "What is most important in my life?" Remember, you are going for states of emotion or feeling. If family or money is what is most important to you, determine the emotions or feelings that you believe that family or money would give you. For each value you identify, determine if the way you live your life conflicts with these values.

Here is an example:

1. What is most important in my life? My wife.
2. My values are those emotional states that I value. Because my wife offers me love and connection, my true values are love and connection.
3. I need to ask myself if there are ways that I live my life that conflict with desire for love and connection. Example: I get defensive when she is upset with me.

Day 9

Beliefs

In Day 8, you identified your values. Today, you will identify your core beliefs that may be conflicting with that which you value.

Ultimately, the resistance that we experience in our lives is due to the conflicting beliefs that we hold. Frequently, just by identifying the belief that is generating resistance will automatically lead to that belief losing its potency. The following exercise is for identifying the beliefs behind your resistance.

Daily Exercise:

Make a list of the situations in your life that are causing you conflict or making you frustrated. When writing your items for your list, expand upon them so that you have a clear understanding of what is involved.   Example: Instead of listing your spouse, write "When my spouse criticizes me." You will use this list in the exercise for day 10.

Day 10

Accessing your beliefs

When you have completed your list, choose the item that is most important for you to address. When you have selected your item, I want you to rephrase your item by rewording it in the following manner: "What does it mean to me_____.I have provided an example of how to approach this exercise by using the problem "I feel angry because my boss is always criticizing me."

1. I reword my problem to read: "What does it mean to me to have my boss criticize me?"

2. I would then respond to that question by writing: "It means that he is unfair."

3. I would then ask myself, "What does it mean to me to that he is unfair?

4. I would respond by saying that "It means he does not appreciate me."

5. I would then ask "What does it mean to me that he does not appreciate me?"

6. I would respond "It means that I am not good enough."

7. I would then ask "What does it mean that I am not good enough?"

8. I would respond with "It means that I am not worthwhile."

You want to continue this line of thinking until you cannot go any further with your questioning.

At the surface level, I believe that I am angry with my boss's criticism. However, the root belief that is causing me problems is that I believe that I am not worthwhile. Because I do not recognize that is my root belief, I become reactive to my boss's behavior. If I truly believed that I was worthwhile, I would find ways to deal with the situation that benefits me and hopefully my boss.

Day 11

Changing a Belief

In this section you will use the belief that you identified in Day 10 and transform it.

Transforming limiting thoughts

Once you have identified your root belief (from the previous exercise), you can change that belief by using the following exercise:

1. Get two sheets of paper. Select paper sizes of 8" x 11" or larger.

2. Take the first sheet of paper and fold it in half lengthwise.

3. On the top of the paper, write down your root belief.

4. Make a list on the left-hand side of the paper of all the ways this belief has cost you in your life. When doing this part of the exercise, think of how this root belief has affected you in all your life areas. Ask yourself how this belief has affected you in the way you see yourself, how it has affected your emotional health, your relationships, your physical health, your work, your finances, and so on.

5. When writing, keep in mind the following:

   • When writing this list, write down the first thing that comes to your mind, even if it seems irrelevant.

   • Write as fast as you can and feel the emotions that arise. This is a heartfelt exercise, not a thinking one.

   • Keep writing until you run out of things to write.

6. By each item that you write down, assign an arbitrary point value as to how much impact

this item has had on you. When selecting the point value, choose the first number that comes to mind.

7. When you have completed assigning the point values, find the total of all the point values and place it at the bottom of the page.

8. For the right side of the page, repeat Steps 6-7, except this time, you will write down all the ways that this belief has benefited you.

When you have completed Step 8, think of a new alternative belief that empowers you. For example, if the original belief was "No one will ever love me," my new belief maybe "The only love that I can depend on is the love that I give to myself."

On the second paper, repeat steps 1-8, using your new belief, with the following exceptions: Reverse Steps 6 and 8 by writing down all the ways that you believe that you would benefit from this new belief for Step 6. When doing Step 8, write down all the ways you believe it will cost you.

When you have completed the two sheets, do the following:

1. Immediately review your lists, allowing yourself to fully experience any emotions that arise.

2. Review your lists every day, once in the morning and once before you go to bed until you become fully associated with the emotions that you experience.

When you become fully associated with the costs for holding on to your old belief with the benefits of adopting your new belief, your mind will become programmed with your new belief.

Day 12

Preparing for Change

In this exercise, you will make list of actions that you can take that are consistent with your new empowering belief that you created in the last exercise. Here is an example:

- My old root belief was that "I am not worthy."
- My new belief (developed through the day 11 exercise) is "I am worthy just by the fact that I exist."

For today's exercise, I made a list all the actions that I could take to demonstrate that I am worthy. For example:

- Treat myself to a fancy dinner.
- Honor my feelings and spend the day doing only what I want to do.
- Go on that trip that I always wanted to take.

When your list is complete, I want you to schedule a time and date when you will commit to doing those actions that you have selected from your list.

Day 13 & 14

Acceptance and Resistance

Because we experience ourselves as having a mind and body, we experience ourselves as being separate from the rest of the world. Given that we experience ourselves as being separate, we resist those aspects of our experience that we find painful, such as certain thoughts or sensations.

Someone who had a bad relationship may resist experiencing thoughts of that relationship or the sensations (feelings and emotions) of their lingering pain. When we resist our thoughts and sensations, we cut ourselves off from the deeper aspects of us. We cut ourselves off from our connection with pure consciousness by identifying with the thoughts and sensations that we are avoiding. If we did not identify with our painful thoughts and sensations, we would not resist them, allowing us to focus on silence and the nature of awareness.

The power of acceptance is that it allows us to release our resistance and our identification to that which we are resisting. I stated earlier that we attract those thoughts that are consistent with our sense of self. If we are resisting any aspect of ourselves, what that we really doing is placing our focus on that which we do not want. We cannot resist anything without being vigilant of it.

By learning to accept our experiences, we reduce our attachment to them. When I speak about acceptance, it does not mean going against how we feel about a situation and pretend that it does not matter. Rather, acceptance means acknowledging the existence of the situation and not fighting against it. Once we accept a situation, we can place our focus on that which we desire.

One of the ways we create resistance in our lives is to go against those things that we value for our lives. If I value love and connection but become defensive, when I feel vulnerable, I am being resistant to that which I value. The following exercise will help you identify those areas in your life where there is a conflict in your values.

Daily Exercise:

Another way we create resistance within ourselves is to agree to do things, which go against how we genuinely feel. This next exercise addresses this.

Schedule a day where you will commit to doing only those things that you feel good about. This exercise is difficult for many people because we are so conditioned to being responsible by our parents and society. We believe that to have self-worth we need to be responsible and meet the expectations of others. If you have trouble with this exercise, doing it for less than a day and gradually increase the period of time till you can do it for a full day.

You may be thinking that this exercise is unrealistic. After all, there are things that we all have to do which we rather avoid. The focus of this exercise has less to do with the task at hand and more about the resistance that we are experiencing. Should there be something that requires your attention, of which you are experiencing resistance, your goal is to lower your resistance before you engage in that task. The following are steps for lowering your resistance.

1. Think about the benefits of doing the task and the consequences of not doing it. If the benefits of completing the tasks outweigh the consequences of not doing it, you should feel less resistance doing the task.
2. Think of how you could change your approach to doing the tasks in a manner that makes doing it more enjoyable. Example: If you need to pull weeds from your garden, listen to your favorite music as you are weeding.
3. If none of the previous suggestions change the way you feel about the task, postpone

doing the task until you come to point where you can do it with acceptance.

Week 3

Focus: The Mind's Sword for cutting through Obstacles

In the last two chapters, we have covered the nature of silence, of consciousness, of experience, and of thoughts and beliefs. With the exception of experience, most of us associate these topics with the mind. In many teachings of meditation, we are told that the goal is to achieve a "silent mind." We also believe that consciousness, thoughts, and beliefs are contained in the mind.

As for the mind, many spiritual teachings make out the mind to be our enemy, that it impedes the attainment of enlightenment.

We are far enough into this book that I feel ready to expose another illusion that most of us have bought into. There is no mind. The mind does not exist. The mind is just another concept that we have created. Just as you have a psychological self, you also have a "mind" that the psychological self believes in. Both your psychological self and your mind are thoughts that we, as a species, have believed into existence.

That most of the human race has a conviction that they are a physical body with a mind is a testament to the power of beliefs. That which we believe becomes our reality and the belief in the existence of a mind is no different. What we believe to be a mind is the attraction of thoughts to our most fundamental thought, the psychological self.

Because of our deep-seated conviction of having a mind, it is easier to work with the mind to transcend it than it is to go fight against it. As we reach higher levels of awareness, it will eventually become self-evident that neither our minds nor our psychological selves are real. We learn to accept their existence, as illusionary aspects, without becoming attached to or personalizing them. Like anything else that we experience, the mind is just another object in awareness, which is our essential self.

The power of our minds is infinite, though the mind itself is illusionary. It is infinite it is power because it is a projection of consciousness that mirrors the infinite potential of consciousness. When we personalize our mind by believing that it is who we are, we are like the servant who unquestionably serves their master. When you create distance between you and your mind and can observe it, then you are moving in the direction where your mind becomes the servant of you.

The ability to become the masters of our own minds, and transcend to higher levels of consciousness, is purely the function of our ability to control our focus. The ability to control our focus is the center of all teachings, be they metaphysical or not. Whether it is solving a math problem or transcending thought, it is our ability to direct our attention that makes it possible to expand consciousness. Ultimately, it is the redirecting of attention away from objects and toward awareness itself that leads to true freedom. For this book, I define true freedom as the ability to transcend the perceived limitations that are imposed by the identification with the mind and body.

In the following days of this week, you will learn ways that you can use your focus to improve the quality of your life by transcending the sense of limitation that is imposed by our belief in the mind.

Day 15

Problem Solving

Albert Einstein once said, "No problem can be solved from the same level of consciousness that created it." All problems that we experience are a result of our own thinking. The flaw in our thinking that leads to humanity's problems is that we see ourselves as being separate from others. Because everything in life is interconnected, we create problems when we ignore the interconnectedness of life.

Our inability to perceive the interconnectedness of life is not limited to our relationships with those around us. It also extends to our inability to perceive our interconnectedness with our essential selves. Because of this ignorance, we find ourselves being swayed by our limited beliefs. Examples of such beliefs include:

- "It can't be done."

- "That idea is impossible."
- "I need to be realistic.
- "I will never figure this out."
- "It is too hard."
- "I have tried everything."
- "This always happens to me."
- "I am not smart enough."
- "I can't figure it out."
- "I give up."

As stated earlier, the thoughts that we hold attract other thoughts of like kind. One way to practice problem-solving from higher levels of consciousness is through the use of intention and silence. There are basic steps to problem-solving from higher levels of awareness:

- Silence
- Intention
- Detachment

Silence: We can achieve a state of mental calm by going into meditation, being out in nature, physical exercise, or whatever works for you. However you reach it, you want to enter a state where you are feeling calm yet alert. Of all the ways to do this, the practice of meditation is most effective.

Intention: When you have reached the state of mental calm, express your intention to yourself with a sense of certainty. It is important that you believe that your intention is possible. If you harbor doubt, that is what will be communicated to the larger consciousness system. Examples of intentions would be:

- I have the job that I desire.
- I am healing my relationship.
- I am becoming stronger.
- I am overcoming this challenge.
- The solution to my problem will appear when the time is right.
- The solution to my problem exists already; I just need to be ready to receive it.

- I am enjoying the process of discovering the solution to my problem.
- It feels good to know that I am learning to access higher levels of awareness for problem solving.

Notice that these examples are not all directed at achieving the final answer to the problem. Some of these intentions are process oriented rather than results oriented. If you find yourself harboring any doubts of achieving your intention, go with a process-oriented intention.

Example:

- Outcome-oriented: I am healing my relationship.
- Process oriented: I am enjoying learning about my relationship.

Whether your intentions are process oriented or results oriented does not matter, both will get you to your answer when the time is right for you to receive the answer.

When formulating your intentions, observe the following criteria:

- They must be sincere and heartfelt.
- The outcome of your intentions needs to benefit all those who are impacted by your intentions.
- They need to be stated in the positive.
- They need to be stated in the present tense.

Detachment

Once you have communicated your intention, the next step is to practice detachment. Detachment means placing your focus on something that is unrelated to solving your problem. If you continue to focus on getting the answer to your problem, you will risk becoming disappointment or experience doubt. Since the vibrational level of your doubt or disappointment will be stronger than your trust in the manifestation process, your answer will remain elusive. The best formula for detachment is to become silent, release your intention, and get on with your life!

Daily Exercise:

Make a list of intentions that you have which would be meaningful you, if you could make them your reality. Be sure to craft them as described in this section. You will use your list in Day 16.

Day 16

Manifestation

For the rest of this week, practice the manifestation process using your list from Day 15. Follow the steps that you learned in Day 15:

1. Become silent (using meditation is recommended).
2. Express your intention silently to yourself.
3. Practice detachment.

When doing this exercise, do not get involved in the outcome that you experience. In other words, do not get disappointed if your intentions do not manifest right away. In the beginning, just focus on the process. Your intentions will manifest as you learn to develop your sense of acceptance for whatever appears in your life.

Day 17 & 18

Visualizations

Visualizing is great for accessing and influencing the subconscious. Visualization is also a valuable tool for turning your intentions into reality. However, there are aspects of the visualizing process that are often misunderstood. The following are some key points to consider when visualizing:

1. There is an abundance of visualizing programs available on the market, and they can be useful if you have never visualized before. However, the most effective visualizations occur when you create your own visualizations. Once you understand the process, learn to trust your imagination and just go with it.

2. Many people feel they are unable to visualize, as they are unable to develop clear

images in their mind. Do not worry about the quality of your images. However you experience your visualizations, trust them. Some people are unable to see images; rather, they experience sensations. With continued practice, your visualizations will become more vivid.

3. Before visualizing, it's helpful to formulate an intention for yourself. Examples of intentions would be:

    a. Visualizing your desires already manifested

    b. Visualizing yourself exploring that which you are resisting.

    c. Visualizing you taking on a new challenge as a form of a mental rehearsal.

    d. Visualizing you solving a problem.

Daily Exercise:

Practice incorporating the visualization process into this week's lesson of manifesting your intentions. **Note:** While you want to remain dethatched from your intentions, you still can visualize them. When we are attached to our intentions, we are thinking about how or when they will manifest. When we visualize our intentions, we are focusing on the intention itself, not how or when it will occur.

Day 19

Changing Perception

Most of us experience the world through our perspective of life. The ability to step into the perspective of another is a powerful tool for creating empathy and understanding with the people in our life.

1. Think about the person whose perspective you want to enter.
2. When thinking about this person, think of their frustrations and concerns that they have and the reasons for it. You do not have to understand or even agree with their perspective; your job is to just recognize their frustrations.
3. Announce to yourself your intention to enter this person's perspective.
4. Enter your meditation, reminding yourself again of your intention.

5. When you reach a calm mental state, repeat the intention one last time. From this point on, do make any attempts to influence your experience or hold any expectations. Simply remain open and allow whatever you experience to present itself.

6. Practice by repeating this exercise until you experience the perceptive of the other person.

Like most of the exercises provided in this book, this exercise takes practice. Do not get disappointed if this exercise did not work for you. It takes time to recondition our minds to successfully to this exercise. When you can get this exercise to work for you, try it out with animals!

Week 4

Feelings and Emotions: Messengers from the Universe

Our feelings and emotions play a major role the development of higher levels of awareness by providing us with feedback to our alignment with our essential self. You and I are multidimensional beings in that we are both non-phenomenal and phenomenal. Our essential self is non-phenomenal while our manifested form is phenomenal. What is referred to as "enlightenment" is when our phenomenal self becomes aligned with our non-phenomenal self.

What cause us to get out of alignment are the thoughts and beliefs that we identify with. There are two stages of the alignment process. The first stage is alignment that results from focusing on those thoughts that empower and support us in our happiness. The second stage is when we transcend all thoughts and focus on awareness itself. This section focuses largely on the first stage; many of Week 1's exercises addressed the second stage.

Emotions are the palpable expression of thoughts; they are a mirror to our thoughts. The quality of our emotions that we experience reflects the thoughts that we are placing our attention on. If you are angry it is because you are focusing on angry thoughts. If you are feeling peaceful, it is because you are focusing on peaceful thoughts. We can improve our alignment with pure consciousness by identifying those thoughts that are causing us unhappiness. Sometimes it is difficult to identify our thoughts that are causing us unhappiness, especially when those thoughts are subconscious. By noticing the quality of our emotions, we can readily identify the thoughts that are behind them.

Unlike our emotions, our feelings are not a reflection of thoughts. Rather, they are an indicator to our alignment with pure conscious. While our feelings are our primary indicator to our alignment, our emotions are a secondary indicator of alignment. Emotions only indicate the quality of our thoughts. I recommend that you read through these meditations first before practicing it. Or, record them on audio tape and play it back as you do this exercise.

Day 20

Observing Sensations

The sensations of the body, both pleasant and an unpleasant, inform us of whether we are in alignment with the highest aspect of ourselves. This exercise will help you become more aware of the sensations of your body.

1. Close your eyes and allow yourself to follow your breath during inhalation and exhalation. Place your attention on your breath. Feel it as it courses through your body.

2. Now place your attention on the sensations of the body. Place your attention on any sensation of the body that appears in your awareness.

3. Do you feel a tingling in your hands or feet? Do you feel tension in your back, shoulders, or face? Do you feel the weight of your body or the pressure on your buttocks from the chair or ground that you are sitting on?

4. Allow yourself to experience the sensations of the body without any judgment of any of them, even the ones that may feel unpleasant. Sensations are just that sensations, there are no good or bad sensations. Good and bad, pleasant and unpleasant, these are value judgments that exist solely in mind. The same thing is true with perceptions, sounds, and thoughts; they just are.

5. Are the sensations that you experience stable? Are they always the same or do they

change? Are they always there or do they come and go?

6. Just stay in the awareness of your body's sensation, allow yourself to experience them for as long as you desire.

7. This is the end of this meditation; feel free to allow yourself to continue to meditate on the body for as long as you wish.

Day 21

Observing Emotions

This next meditation is about observing your emotions. To observe your emotions is to be aware of them. You can transform your emotions by simply being aware of them as well inquiring about their qualities.

1. Sit down in a comfortable position and close your eyes.

2. Allow yourself to follow your breath during inhalation and exhalation. Place your attention on your breath. Feel it as it courses through your body.

3. Have complete acceptance for whatever you experience during this meditation.

4. Observe the perceptions, thoughts, sensations, feelings, and emotions that arise

within you. Allow them to come and go on their own accord. All you need to do is be the observer of them.

5. Now pay attention to any emotion that arises. Become an observer of it, what happens when your focus is placed on your emotion?

6. Do not place any meaning on the emotion you experience; do not think of it as being positive or negative. Words such as "positive", "negative," "pleasant," or "unpleasant" are products of the mind

7. There is no intrinsic meaning to anything in life. All meaning is derived from our minds. Emotions and feelings have no power of their own; they derive all their power from the attention we give them.

8. When observing emotions, do so with complete allowing; do not try to change anything about it.

9. As you observe your emotions, do you notice a change in how you experience them? Do they change in intensity? Do they become stronger or milder? Can you locate where they come from? Can you observe where they go?

10. As you observe emotions, ask yourself "Am I my emotions or am I the one that is aware of them?" If a feeling or emotion is experienced as being unpleasant, does awareness feel unpleasant? If an emotion is experienced as being pleasant, does awareness feel this pleasant?

11. Awareness does not experience anything; awareness only elucidates experience. Awareness is like a beam of light shining on

a snow-covered field. The light does not feel the cold of the snow; it only illuminates it. As you observe emotions, be as the beam of light.

12. This is the end of this meditation. Feel free to remain in meditation for as long as you wish.

Transforming Sensations

Using awareness, you can not only develop your powers of discernment but to also transform what you focus on. In this exercise, you will transform your experience of sensations.

1. Sit down and make yourself comfortable, if you like, you can close your eyes.
2. Place your attention on your breath as it travels in and out of your body. Allow your awareness to wash over your body and experience the sensations of the body.

3. Now scan your body with your awareness for a relaxed, calm, or pleasant sensation. When you find such a sensation, allow yourself to focus on it.

4. As you observe this sensation, I want you to ask yourself the following question: "What color is this sensation?" Accept the first response that comes to mind.

5. Now ask "What size is this sensation?" Again, go with the first answer that comes to mind.

6. Now ask yourself "Does this sensation have a texture to it? Is it smooth, rough, soft, or hard?"

7. Now search the body for a sensation that is not relaxed, calm, or pleasant. Perhaps it has a tension, pressure, heaviness, or hardness to it.

8. Now just as with the pleasant sensation, ask yourself: "What are the color, size, and texture of this sensation?"

9. Now using your awareness, allow yourself to imagine that the qualities of the unpleasant sensation take on the qualities of the pleasant sensation. If the pleasant sensation had a green color, imagine the color of the unpleasant sensation changing to green. If the texture of the pleasant sensation was soft, imagine the unpleasant sensation grow soft, and so on.

10. Take your time as you transfer the qualities of the pleasant sensation to the unpleasant sensation.

11. Now observe the unpleasant sensation. Has the sensation changed? Has this sensation develop a more pleasant quality to it? If not, continue to practice this meditation.

12. This is the end of this meditation.

Day 23

Experience Freedom

Most instructions for meditation advise you to sit in a comfortable position while sitting straight in an upright position. One of keys to meditation is learning to be allowing of all experiences, to not control anything. The same is true with the body. In this meditation, you will listen to the body and allow it to move or position itself in complete freedom.

1. Sit down and make yourself comfortable and allow yourself to relax.

2. Close your eyes and focus on your breath, allow yourself to become relaxed.

3. Forget about what you learned from your mother about sitting straight. If your body

feels like slumping over, let it. Allow your body to do whatever it wants.

4. Place your awareness on the body and its sensations. Let your awareness be soft, and do not get caught up in your thinking. Simply observe the sensations of the body and any messages that you are getting from the body.

5. This is the end of this meditation. Please feel free to allow yourself to listen to your body for as long as you desire.

Day 24

Trust your Feelings

Our feelings are informing us to whether we are moving toward or away from our own integrity as a human being. When we do not trust our feelings, we are unable to trust ourselves. This next meditation will involve noting how feelings and sensations are affected by our focus.

1. Sit down, close your eyes, and relax.

2. Allow yourself to become silent and observe the thoughts, feelings, emotions, and sensations that arise within. Allow all of these phenomena to present themselves to your awareness.

3. I want you to think of a situation that is currently causing you feelings of uneasiness, concern, or hurt. When you identify such a

situation, allow yourself to focus on it. Relive the experience in your mind.

4. As you focus on the situation, become aware of the feelings that arise. Allow the feelings to arise naturally. Remember, your feelings are like a compass; they have a message for you. They are telling you to move toward or away from that which you are focusing on. When we are making decisions, taking actions, or focusing on things that bring about pleasant feelings, we know that we are on the right track and are being consistent with our sense of integrity. Conversely, when we have feelings that are unpleasant, we are experiencing situations that are inconsistent with our sense of integrity.

5. Now ask yourself: "What can I do, believe, or focus on that will make me feel better about this situation?" Is there a decision that you need to make? Do you need let go of

something? Do you need to question your thinking? Do you need to take time for yourself? Do you need to risk disappointing others?

6. Keep inquiring with yourself until you have identified a way to address the situation that leaves you feeling a sense of relief, calm, or peace.

7. When you come up with a solution to the situation that feels good to you, trust that this is the correct decision for you. Your feelings are completely accurate and reliable, for you, at this moment of time. If your feelings regarding your solution or the situation change, honor them as well.

8. Be sure not to confuse your feelings for your thoughts or beliefs. Your feelings are reliable; however, your thoughts and beliefs are not.

9. If you are unable to find a way to make yourself feel better, this is okay also. Allow yourself to remain with the feeling. Offer your feeling your full acceptance. Accepting our feelings and being at peace with them is an act of self- love and an indication of integrity.

10. This is the end of the meditation. Please remain in your stillness for as long as you like.

Day 25

Transforming Emotions

This next exercise will involve you playing a more active role than in the previous exercise, and it is a powerful tool if you have a strong negative emotion that has been lingering in you. I recommend that you read through this meditation first before practicing it. Or, record it on audio tape and play it back as you do this exercise.

Do the following:

1. Sit down and make yourself comfortable.
2. Close your eyes and allow yourself to relax
3. Place your attention on your breath as it enters and exits your body, focusing on the sensations you experience as you inhale and exhale.
4. If you are not already experiencing a negative emotion, relive a memory that will activate one. Think of a negative experience from the past or that you are currently experiencing.

5. When the unpleasant emotion arises, identify the emotion. Examples could be anger, fear, concern, sadness, etc.

6. When you have identified the emotion, describe what the emotion feels like. Notice: You want to describe what the emotion feels like, not what you think about it. To avoid falling into this trap, phrase your response as "It feels like_____?

Here are some examples:
- "It feels like it is crushing me."
- "I feel like I want to run away."
- "It leaves me feeling numb."
- "It feels like a boulder crushing me."

1. After you identify what the emotion feels like, repeat this process with the response that you give. Example:
   a. If the emotion that I am feeling is anger, my response to what it feels like is "It feels like my body is tightening."

b. I would then repeat the process by asking "What does the tightening of the body feel like?

c. My response to that could be "It feels like my body is hard."

d. I would follow up with "What does a hard body feel like?"

e. With every response that I give, I would repeat the same line of questioning until the emotion transforms into a positive emotion.

When describing the feeling of the emotion, go by the first answer that comes to you. Do not worry about getting it wrong; you can't. As long as you describe the feeling of the emotion without getting intellectual about it, you will be on the right track. Every time you describe an emotion, you allow it to transform itself. By continuously describing it every time that it transforms, the emotion will eventually transform into a positive emotion. Using this process facilitates the emotion to go full circle and heal itself.

Letting go

There is nothing in your experience that does not arise from within you. We experience the world through perception, sensation, sound, and taste, all of which come from within us. These phenomena simply arise and fade within the space of your awareness on their own accord. So what are you holding onto? What are you trying to control? In this next meditation is about allowing.

1. Sit down and make yourself comfortable, allow yourself to relax. If you would like, you may close your eyes for now.

2. Allow yourself to relax as you focus on your breath, place your attention on your breath as it enters your body, travels through your body, and then leaves it as you exhale.

3. Breathe normally, without exerting any effort. Relax.

4. Allow yourself to develop a sense of total acceptance. Be totaling allowing of what appears in your awareness.

5. Do not judge, evaluate, or analyze anything that you experience.

6. Do not hold any expectations for what you should be experiencing.

7. Do not search for anything. Do not imagine anything. Do not create anything. Simply observe.

8. If unpleasant or uncomfortable thoughts, feelings, or sensation arise, let them be.

9. Allow all of your experiences to come into your awareness. Do not try to change them. Do not

try to replace them with something that is more pleasant or positive.

10. You cannot do anything wrong. What you ever you are experiencing, this is the right experience for you.

11. Simply allow experience to flow through your awareness. Simply observe.

12. There is nothing for you to do. There is nothing for you to change. There is nothing for you to believe. Simply be the observer of all that presents itself.

13. This is the end of this meditation. Allow yourself to remain in silence for as long as you desire.

Day 27

Ω

Challenging Minds and Cultivating Freedom

If you have gone through all the exercises in the previous chapters, congratulations! It shows that you are committed to changing your experience of life and that you are open to new ideas. You may have found the contents in this book difficult to understand. If so, I recommend that you re-read it and repeat the exercises until they start to resonate with you. You do not have to understand everything in this book. Nor do you have to feel successful in all the exercises in order to get the full benefit of this book. When you revisit this book, which I hope you do, I would like you to consider some important points.

- Everything that has been written in this book is something that you do already know. The only difference between our everyday experience and what is described in this book is that our everyday experience is usually attributed to a function of the world around us or a function from within us. If I am caught in a traffic-jam and feel frustrated, I would attribute the situation to all the other drivers on the road and the building frustration that I am feeling. Because I experience myself as a separate entity, I see myself as a victim of my circumstances. After all, my experience of the being caught in traffic is the result of something outside myself, something that I cannot control. The fact that I feel frustrated should be no surprise.

The perspective I am tried to demonstrate to you through this book points to a drastically different understanding. The traffic jam, my experience of myself, my thoughts, perceptions, and sensation, are all objects within the field of awareness. Awareness takes in every possible experience that I could have. The truth of who I am is that awareness. Everything that has been written in this book is pointing to this.

If this perspective seems too extreme that is okay. If any aspect of this book resonates with you, it is my hope you will continue with this exploration. You and I have been operating under the conditioning of society from the time we were born. In turn, all the preceding generations were similarly indoctrinated.

There is nothing wrong with our experience of this world, or the experience we have of ourselves. Our challenge is when we limit ourselves to this perspective and remain unaware of our true potential, which is infinite. The truth of who you are is beyond what your mind can grasp!

- For the reasons just stated, your exercises for the rest of this day is to practice those exercises in this book which feel right for you and review any part of this book that you may remain unclear about. Unless you had an understanding of metaphysics before reading this book, you will most likely have to reread it as there was a lot of information provided.

- Finally, I would like to leave you with one final point. From the introduction, there was the story of the farmer who was looking at the moon. You do not want to confuse the content of this book for what you are really seeking, which is expanded awareness. That which you ultimately desire exists within you already, and it always will. This book is just my way of pointing to it.

The End

Dear reader,

Before you close this book, I want to leave you with one last wish.

Treat these four weeks as an introduction to the nature of consciousness. Make them a part of your daily lifestyle. Practice them and apply them whenever you can as you go through your day.

Finally, if you enjoyed the journey then I´d like to ask you for a favor to leave an honest review on amazon. It´d be greatly appreciated.

Just click here to leave a review on amazon.

Thank you and good luck!

Erik

CPSIA information can be obtained
at www.ICGtesting.com
Printed in the USA
LVHW040027090520
655272LV00004B/1330